The Class Size Debate

The Class Size Debate

Is Small Better?

Peter Blatchford

with Paul Bassett, Harvey Goldstein and Clare Martin, and Gemma Catchpole, Suzanne Edmonds and Viv Moriarty

Open University Press
Maidenhead · Philadelphia

Open University Press
McGraw-Hill Education
McGraw-Hill House
Shoppenhangers Road
Maidenhead
Berkshire
England
SL6 2QL

email: enquiries@openup.co.uk
world wide web: www.openup.co.uk

and

325 Chestnut Street
Philadelphia, PA 19106, USA

First published 2003

A catalogue record of this book is available from the British Library

ISBN 0 335 21162 3 (pb) 0 335 21163 1 (hb)

Library of Congress Cataloging-in-Publication Data
Blatchford, Peter.
The class size debate: is small better? / Peter Blatchford with Paul Bassett . . . [et al.].
p. cm.
Includes bibliographical references and index.
ISBN 0–335–21163–1 — ISBN 0–335–21162–3 (pbk.)
1. Class size—Great Britain—Longitudinal studies. 2. Academic achievement—Great Britain—Longitudinal studies. 3. Education (Elementary)—Great Britain—Longitudinal studies. I. Title.

LB3013.2 .B59 2003
371.2′51—dc21
2002035458

Typeset by RefineCatch Limited, Bungay, Suffolk
Printed in Great Britain by Biddles Ltd, *www.biddles.co.uk*

Contents

Figures, tables and boxes

Figures

Tables

Boxes

Acknowledgements

It is my great pleasure to thank a number of people for their contribution to this book. I want, first of all, to thank my colleagues at the Institute of Education who have worked with me on the Class Size Research Project. Paul Bassett was the statistician, and his analyses have been a model of clarity and rigour. Harvey Goldstein conducted some of the early analyses and gave invaluable advice throughout the project. Clare Martin has been the research officer since the earliest days, and had the unenviable task of organizing and processing the large volume of data. Gemma Catchpole was the research officer on the Key Stage 2 phase of the project. Suzanne Edmonds and Viv Moriarty worked on parts of the project, reported in this book. I would also like to thank my colleagues Peter Kutnick at the University of Brighton and Ed Baines who have worked with me on research into within-class grouping, which has informed some of the text in this book. Although I wrote the text, all these colleagues have contributed, in many important ways, to the project, and have co-authored a number of other papers on which this book is based.

I want to thank Kim Reynolds, who has been the project secretary throughout its life, for her patience, good humour and informed discussions about football (despite an unfortunate affinity for a certain north London football team).

I would also like to thank Peter Mortimore, who was director of the Institute of Education, for his invitation to collaborate with him on a paper for the National Commission for Education, and his support in getting the Class Size Research Project under way.

I would like to give special thanks to the staff in local education authorities (LEAs), and teachers and head teachers in schools, who have worked so hard to provide the information for the project and, of course, to the children in those schools.

The research would not have been possible without the far-sightedness of the participating LEAs, who contributed funds to the early phases of the research, and the Department for Education and Skills (DfES) for funding the last year of the project, which focused on pupil–adult ratios. I would like to thank, particularly, Judy Sebba in the DfES for being a good critical friend of the project and for her incisive chairing of the steering committee, and also to Victoria White for her help. Thanks are also due to the Economic and Social Research Council (ESRC) for funding research on within-class grouping, which was co-directed by Peter Kutnick and myself.

I want also to thank Maurice Galton, Judy Sebba and Jeremy Finn, who gave helpful comments on the book proposal, and to Jim Cobbett, Trish McNamara and Fiz Starkey, who commented on a draft of the manuscript of this book. I have done my best to respond to their helpful comments; they should not be held responsible for any remaining problems, technical or stylistic.

I want to thank Jeremy Finn and Chuck Achilles from the Tennessee STAR project team for showing what could be done in this area, and for their support.

Finally I would like to thank Shona Mullen and Anita West at the Open University Press for their interest and careful handling of the proposal and manuscript.

Peter Blatchford

1 Introduction

There has been a vigorous debate about class sizes in schools. On one side of the debate are the enthusiasts who feel very strongly that smaller classes lead to better teaching and more effective learning. Achilles and Finn (2000: 316) have expressed this point very forcefully: 'Class size [reductions] should not just be a cornerstone, but the foundation of educational policy for . . . early education'. This belief has informed policy in many parts of the world; in the USA, for example, there has been huge investment in class size reductions. On the other side of the debate are the sceptics who argue that the evidence for the efficacy of class size reductions is in doubt and that there are likely to be other more cost-effective strategies for improving educational standards. This book describes a large-scale research project which set out to seek answers to the class size debate. This is not a book which seeks to either proselytize or debunk – rather it seeks to provide a sustained inquiry into the issue, based on a longitudinal study of children's progress over three years after entry into English primary schools. We hope that the book will show the value of research evidence as a main tool in this debate. It is not, though, intended to be exclusively a research report intended for other researchers. Deliberately it is written to be read by all who are interested in this topic: teachers, policy makers in local authorities and government, school governors and parents.

My interest in the class size issue began when Peter Mortimore and I were asked by the National Commission on Education to write a briefing document for them on the educational effects of class size differences (Mortimore and Blatchford 1993). Several things became apparent during our work. In looking at the current facts and figures about class sizes it was clear that there was a problem of large classes at primary level. I do not intend to describe the statistics in detail here (see Blatchford et al. 1998), but it was clear that class sizes were larger on average in primary than in secondary schools. As an example, in 1996 the average class size in England at primary was 27.5 and at secondary level 21.9. This seemed to us to turn on its head what was more sensible educationally – that is, younger children need more support from their teachers. There were a troubling number of classes over 30. Average class sizes over the period 1982–96 increased by 2.1 pupils and more than a quarter of classes in 1996 had more than 30 pupils. International comparisons were available only for pupil–teacher ratios, not class sizes. They showed that pupil–teacher ratios in England and Wales compared very unfavourably with many other industrialized countries

The second thing that became apparent was the consensus among many in education that smaller classes allowed a better quality of teaching and learning. To give a concrete illustration of this let us look at this summary of an observer's report after a visit made to a small infant school class of just 15 pupils.

General atmosphere

There was lightness about the activities and a good deal of humour. The teacher joked with the children (for example, comments were made at her daughter's expense concerning her propensity to hoard and store things in the loft), chatted to the observer, discussed social things with the children. It was not that work was neglected, rather it was supported by a personal style of interaction. The teacher was able to maintain a running and public commentary on children's work.

Classroom control

There was a very noticeable contrast with the situation in another school visited at about the same time by the same observer, involving a teacher in a large class of over 30. While the teacher in the small class spent little time on control, and there was little need to keep children on-task, in the large class interactions with the children largely involved a constant battle to keep children's attention on-task. As a consequence the teacher was severe, and the children subdued.

Teaching interactions

The teacher of the small class was able to stay with one small group (whom she felt needed her help) for more or less the whole session. They received sustained attention and she was able to offer immediate feedback. Task allocation and preparation was very deliberate, responsive and individualized; she went through each person in turn and asked what they wanted to do from a list of activities and she then set them off.

Knowledge of children

The teacher felt that the main advantage of having a small class was that she knew children individually, and that this informed her teaching, for example in terms of questions to children, she was aware of who knew and did not know something.

Support for reading

The teacher felt very strongly that hearing children of this age read individually in school was important. The small class allowed almost daily sessions in which there was a stress on individualized support at this crucial time in children's reading development. This would not be possible in a larger class.

It is easy on the basis of this account to see why teachers would feel that 'small is better'. Obviously there are questions about the generalizability of individual case descriptions. Characteristics of the children in the school, the composition of the class, qualities of the teacher and the school, all will be important. But this description of the situation in one class serves to show the obvious potential in smaller classes for more teaching support and more focused teaching. In visits to schools it was clear that the overwhelming professional judgement of teachers was that smaller classes allow more effective and flexible teaching and the potential for more effective learning. This is a view widely held by head teachers and school governors (Bennett 1996). This is also probably the view of most parents. It is often cited as one reason why parents pay to send their children to private schools.

But the intriguing thing – and this was the third thing that became apparent from our work – is that when we reviewed the research literature on the educational effects of class size differences (Blatchford and Mortimore 1994), we could find little support for this view.

More precisely, there had been little research conducted on this topic in the UK, and, oddly, that which existed tended to show if anything that children did better academically as class size increased. Perhaps tellingly, an often quoted study by Shapson et al. (1980) in Canada indicated that although teachers felt that their teaching changed for the better in smaller classes, this was not supported by systematic observations of the teachers.

We read all the books and papers we could find on this topic. Some early research, for example, the case studies described by Cahen et al. (1983), still make compelling reading. Overall, however, we concluded that previous research did not have designs strong enough to draw reliable conclusions about the educational effects of class size difference (Blatchford et al. 1998). Despite the importance of the class size issue, and the strength of the popular view in favour of smaller classes, research had little to say about whether class size differences affected children's educational achievements, and still less to say about whether they affected classroom processes, including teaching and pupil behaviour. There was therefore a wide gap between professional experience, which was that smaller classes are better educationally, and research evidence, which was not clear. A main impetus for the research reported in this book was an attempt to bridge this gap.

I also had a personal interest in research on class size differences. At the time that we were planning the research my own daughter was in a large class of 32 in an infant school. I was a parent governor of the school and discussions inevitably covered school budgets and class sizes. As an educational researcher I wanted to inform the discussion by showing what the evidence told us about the educational effects of class size differences, so this could be considered alongside consideration of the financial implications of class sizes. It was extremely frustrating not to be able to offer anything substantial to policy decisions. It seemed to me that, in this regard, educational research had failed to address one of the most important issues of the day.

Political and educational context of the time

I would like to say a bit more about how the research was started. This is often left out of research reports but is helpful in showing the reasoning behind the kind of research we felt was necessary.

One factor that was important in the early stages of the research was the views of politicians and policy makers in the mid-1990s about class size differences. Conservative education ministers of the day, no doubt fearing the cost implications, were unwilling to agree that class size mattered.

> I do not believe there is any proven connection between class size and quality of Education.
>
> (Eric Forth, Minister of State for Education, reported in *The Independent*, 3 March 1993)

The preferred view, supported by an Ofsted report on the class size issue in 1995 (Ofsted 1995a), was that it was the quality of teaching that was more important.

This incensed and energized a number of people in schools, local educational authorities and the teacher associations who objected to the view that class size did not matter and it was all down to individual teachers. It seemed that the research evidence, or rather the lack of it, was allowing politicians to make claims in support of inactivity over large classes. Peter Mortimore and I spoke at a number of meetings during this period to discuss our review and wrote articles published in the educational and political press. It became clear that there was a desire for a proper and thorough study of the educational consequences of class size differences. Senior LEA officials expressed interest in the possibility of research and organized meetings where we spoke with head teachers and others about our plans. I was impressed with the general agreement that any research in this area, to be of value, would need to be long term. It would need to follow children from school entry for at least the first two years of their schooling. There was also general agreement that the focus should be not only on the links between class size and children's educational attainments, but also on *why* class sizes made a difference. As we shall see, the widely quoted Tennessee STAR project had by this time begun to show the benefits of small classes on children's attainment, but could offer no insights into what might explain this finding.

Our study took a long time to set up. We explored a number of options. Eventually it became apparent that if spread between enough LEAs, and in conjunction with the Institute of Education, it would just be possible to raise enough funds to conduct the long-term research it was agreed was required. Later on, after a change of government, we were able to get a grant from the Department for Education and Employment (DfEE, as it was then called) to take the children through to the end of Key Stage 1 (KS1) and also to look more closely at the effect of teaching assistants (TAs) and pupil–teacher and pupil–adult ratios on children's educational progress. (Note: the terms used to describe the first three years of schooling in England and Wales (4–7 years) have changed since the study began. The first year of school – the Reception year – is now part of the Foundation Stage, and the second and third years, that is, Year 1 and Year 2, now make up Key Stage 1. I retain the use of the term 'Reception' in this book.)

Despite the worries of some researchers I want to emphasize that at no time was there any constraint or influence from LEAs or the DfES on the aims or scope of the research. There was general support for the view that to be of any value this had to be an independent study. The LEAs in particular were helpful in providing information and access to schools where they could.

The current debate about class size

Politically, in some countries at least, the policy tide has changed in favour of small classes. Current government policy is for a maximum class size of 30 at Reception and KS1 in England, as well as extra funding for teaching assistants (TAs) in classrooms. In the USA, the US Department of Education launched a seven-year initiative to lower class sizes in the early school grades to an average of 18 students. By July 2000 the US Congress had supported this effort for two years in a row and $2.5 million had been invested. This allowed the employment of around 29,000 additional teachers (foreword to Wang and Finn 2000). Class size reductions have been implemented by a number of US states, most notably in California where large funds were made available. The

California Class Size Reduction Program is probably the single largest state-sponsored educational reform in United States history, with nearly 2 million kindergarten to grade 3 students across the state experiencing reduced class sizes by the reform's third year (Bohrnstedt et al. 2000). There have been initiatives involving class size or pupil to adult ratio reductions in the Netherlands, and in Asia Pacific countries as diverse as New Zealand and China. In China, the *Xinmin Evening News* (8 December 1999) reported that there had been a reduction in class sizes following the Shanghai Education Commission call for a reduction in 1997. The Shanghai Education Commission was also reported to be planning to establish 100 small class experimental schools in 2000 (*Liberation Daily*, 13 February 2000). In Taiwan too, the '410 Education Reform League' has called for smaller classes (Pan and Yu 1999).

Despite these developments there is still considerable disagreement about the cost-effectiveness of class size reductions. Some academics have argued that academic gains from class size reductions are modest at best (Slavin 1989), and funds would be better spent on other educational initiatives. One of the main critics, Eric Hanushek, has concluded on the basis of a review of the evidence that there is little reason to believe smaller classes improve student educational performance (Hanushek 1999) and has argued (Rivkin et al. 2000) against class size reductions in favour of funds being spent on teacher training. Given the continued debate it is therefore understandable if policy makers in a number of countries are keen to establish what the evidence has to say.

The case for a study of class size differences in the mid-1990s was strong; it is my belief that it is still strong today. A major conference in the USA on class size effects concluded that '*An important conclusion that emerged . . . is that the current knowledge base about small classes is limited*' (Wang and Finn 2000: 366; italics in original). This applies with greater force to the UK. It needs to be recognized that, even after moves to limit class sizes to a maximum of 30 in a class at KS1, there is still a lot of variability in class sizes. Many teachers would consider that 29 children in a class, especially when only 5–7 years of age, is still too many. The policy is also still contentious, with opposition parties claiming that class sizes overall have increased. The Liberal Democrat policy at the time of the 2001 election was that the government should go further and reduce the maximum class size to 25 children.

Perhaps the most important reason why research is still needed on class size effects, however, is that we still do not have research evidence that allows us to *understand* any effects of class size differences on children's educational attainments. As well as the relevance of research to decisions about educational resourcing there are also important implications for educational practice. Given that class sizes will inevitably vary from school to school and area to area (even when they may be getting smaller overall), it is important to study how the number of children in the classroom affect teaching and learning, and to use this information to offer advice to teachers.

What is class size?

In order to study the effect of class sizes it is first important to be clear about what it is. Although this may appear straightforward – what could be more obvious than the number of children in a class? – in practice there are a number of complications. In the past there has been a tendency to use the most obvious and available measures, but these are not always the most reliable or precise and it is possible that this has contributed to the generally inconclusive findings from research.

There are two main indicators. Class size in the countries of the UK is measured on the basis of a snapshot of classes taught during an allotted period during one school day. It gives information on the number of children taught in classes with one teacher and with more than one teacher. Pupil–teacher ratios (PTRs) are calculated by dividing the number of pupils on a school's roll by the full-time equivalent number of qualified teachers, excluding short-term cover and teachers who are absent for a term or more. PTRs are different from class size because they take no account, for example, of non-contact time. All the children on roll are divided by all the teachers in the school. It should not be assumed, therefore, that teachers entered into the calculation are teaching for the whole time. Consequently, the pupil element in the PTR is a smaller figure than in the class size figures, and in this sense PTR figures can be misleading.

PTRs are important from an administrative or economic point of view because they are closely related to the amount of money spent per child. However, from a psychological point of view, related more to what children learn, the number of pupils physically present and interacting with each other and the teacher is more important. Although class size figures are therefore probably more helpful as a guide to what pupils experience in schools, figures on PTRs are commonly given, and for some purposes class sizes are not available. International comparisons appear to be available only in terms of PTRs. In the UK, comparisons between the maintained and the independent (fee-paying) sector are also available only in terms of PTRs.

There are other important limitations with measures of class size. First, they are taken from a survey of the number of children supposed to be in a class at one point in time. An accurate account of the number of pupils for whom a teacher has responsibility might seem to be the closest one could get to a class size figure. But the extent to which this figure actually matches the everyday experience of pupils and teachers may be questioned. The number of children actually in the class at any time may be different from the number according to the class register; children may be absent, for example, and the extent of absences may vary from school to school. Moreover, over the course of the school year the number of children may change. This is particularly true of the first year of primary schooling in England – the Reception class. Entry procedures vary from school to school and between LEAs. Sometimes all children enter at the beginning of the school year in which they become 5 years old (in September). Sometimes entry will be termly so that classes may grow in size over the year, or rearranged each time. And sometimes the younger children will start on a part-time basis, only gradually building up to full-time attendance. Once children move beyond the Reception year and there is more stability in class sizes, the actual number present at one time can still vary between lessons, for example, because some may go out of the classroom for certain purposes. There is therefore a distinction between the theoretical class size, that is, the number of children on a register, and what might be called the 'experienced' class size.

These limitations in published class sizes are not trivial; a measure of class size must be closely tied to a child's experience if it is to be precise enough to be examined in relation to educational progress.

Class size and extra staff and adults

Another factor that complicates matters still more is that taking only the teacher into account when considering the effects of class size can be misleading. These days in primary schools there are likely to be many other adults – classroom assistants, learning support assistants (LSAs) and so on, as well as parents and community helpers. The generic term preferred by the UK government for those employed by the school is 'teaching assistant'; in the UK, since the late 1990s there has been a major drive to increase their numbers in schools. So we also need to consider the presence, role and effects of adults other than the teacher in a classroom.

It might therefore be more realistic to calculate a child to adult ratio (where adults would include teaching and support staff) but this would assume that non-teaching staff were equivalent to teaching staff – an assumption that many educational professionals would challenge.

The issue of teaching assistants in classrooms is currently very controversial in the UK. Teaching unions are uneasy about what they see as a possible devaluation of the teacher's role, worrying that there is an assumption that teaching can be done by people with less training and fewer qualifications. In our research we felt that it was important to ask if extra adults in the class *do* make a difference and, if so, in what ways.

In this respect in the STAR project in the USA, small classes were compared with regular classes with and without a full-time teacher aide. We know that children in small classes performed better academically than the other two groups, but the researchers were also able to establish whether teacher aides in regular classes (22–25 pupils) helped to compensate for any negative effects of being in a larger class. Their results were clear: there were no improvements in children's behaviour or academic progress in classes with a teacher aide. Indeed, in some classes children's behaviour was poorer in classes with aides. It was concluded that teaching assistants were not a substitute for the benefits provided by reduced class size (Finn et al. 2000).

It is difficult, though, to generalize these findings to other countries where the experience, training and deployment of teaching assistants may be very different. We felt that it was important to look at the separate effects of class size and extra staff and also whether extra support may be more important in larger classes. Is a class of 30 with two adults equivalent to two small classes of 15? It may be, for example, that the strongest relationships are between pupil–teacher ratios and attainment, rather than just class size. If this is proved to be the case, it would suggest that it is not only or just the number of children in the class that is important but also the numbers of trained teachers. Alternatively it may be that there are stronger connections with outcomes for the more inclusive measure of staff–pupil ratio (that is, all staff paid by the school, such as teaching assistants, as well as teachers). If so, this will have rather different implications for decisions about class sizes and staffing. It is also possible that extra staff will not add anything to the correlation between size of class and outcomes, which would raise questions about how effectively staff are being used. This bears directly on recent government legislation on increasing the number of teaching assistants. We were therefore interested in the deployment of these staff in classrooms and whether their presence affected children's attainments and educational experiences.

Class size as a classroom contextual influence

As well as being under-researched and studies limited in terms of methods, there has been little attempt to conceptualize, or develop theories to account for, the effects of class size differences on teachers and pupils. In particular, how should we consider class size as a factor in relation to teaching and learning?

Main traditions of research on classroom processes, including studies of teaching effectiveness and pupil behaviour, have in common a lack of interest in classroom contextual influences on teaching. There is an underlying assumption of a direct model, where teaching affects, in a causal way, pupils' achievements and learning. But a main principle of our study, and this book, is the view that teachers do not meet pupils out of context, and class size can be seen as one contextual influence on classroom life, to which teachers and pupils will inevitably have to adapt, and which will affect the nature of the interactions between teachers and pupils.

The roots of this view can be found in Bronfenbrenner (1979) and the ecological psychology approach of Barker (1968) and Kounin and Gump (1974). The basic idea is that within the school there will be smaller contexts, such as the playground and especially the classroom, which have qualitatively different sets of relationships, rules and dynamics (Pellegrini and Blatchford 2000). Different class sizes may well involve different dynamics, that influence both teachers and pupils.

Aims of the Institute of Education class size study

Our study was ambitious. It set out to provide the most complete analysis to date of the educational consequences of class size differences, and in so doing to solve the puzzling gap between professional experience and research findings.

Specifically it had two aims:

1. to establish whether class size differences and pupil–adult ratios affect pupils' academic achievement
2. to study connections between class size and classroom processes which might explain any differences in attainment found. As we shall see, we looked at several main processes: within class grouping practices, teaching, individual support for reading, pupil concentration and peer relations.

In Chapter 2 I describe the rationale behind the study and identify its main features. Here I note that, in contrast to the STAR project, we deliberately decided to use a non-experimental design. In other words, rather than assign children and teachers to different class sizes, we decided to measure the effects of natural variations in class size. We did this with a longitudinal follow-up study of children from school entry into Reception classes at 4 years of age, through for the first three years of schooling. We deliberately combined quantitative and qualitative methods, and made use of a multi-method approach to data collection, in which case studies and teacher reports were combined with systematic observations, teacher time allocation estimates and teacher ratings of child behaviour. The aim was to provide an integrated and comprehensive account of how class size affects classroom learning and behaviour.

This book

My aim in this book is to draw the various components of the study into an accessible and integrated account. As far as possible I have avoided jargon and technical details. Much of the discussion in the chapters that follow rests on analyses that have been reported in academic journal papers. Citations for these will be given in the text (they can be found in the References) and can be followed up if desired. I am very keen to make educational research accessible and not consigned to academic journals. Educational research has had a poor reputation which is not entirely undeserved. Perhaps a main defence of its value is to seek to show that it can inform educational topics in a distinctive way that complements the everyday experiences of practitioners, and can help inform policy and practice. In this sense research is not more or less credible than the experiences of, for example, teachers, but it is a different and complementary kind of evidence. It is important that we learn lessons from both.

It might be useful to say what the book will not attempt to cover. It will not go into the economic analysis of class size reductions, for example, in terms of their cost-effectiveness, and it will not go into the more macro-level issues connected to government and local authority budgeting. Our study was not set up to address issues in these areas, but was designed with a focus on the educational or pedagogical issues connected to class size differences.

In this book I look at relations between class size and classroom processes in Chapters 3 to 6. In Chapter 3 I examine connections between class size and within-class groupings, in Chapter 4 I look at class size and teaching, in Chapter 5 class size and individual support for reading, and in Chapter 6 class size and pupil concentration and peer relations. In Chapter 7 the role and effects of teaching assistants in classrooms is explored, and in Chapter 8 the overall relationships between class size and students' achievement are presented. Finally, in Chapter 9 the main themes from each of the separate chapters are highlighted and conclusions drawn about ways in which class size affects educational experiences and progress. The implications for practice and professional development and training are discussed, as well as the sometimes provocative implications for policy.

In the next chapter I describe the limitations of previous research and the way it informed our decisions about our research approach.

2 The Institute of Education class size study

Research approach and methods

Deciding that research was required and fundable, and deciding on the research aims, was a big first step but what kind of study would be most effective? In this chapter I describe the reasoning behind our research approach. As we shall see, this is informed by lessons that we drew from previous research on class size effects. I shall show how it differs from previous work and identify its main features. The chapter ends with a description of schools, classes and children involved in the study and the methods of data collection. While this chapter could be omitted by those readers who want to move immediately to the results, it will provide information to better understand and make judgements about the findings. At the very least the reader may want to refer back to this chapter to access information on the nature of the data we collected.

Previous research on class size differences

In several reviews my colleagues and I have critically examined previous research (Blatchford and Mortimore 1994; Blatchford and Martin 1998; Blatchford et al. 1998). Though rather simplistic, it is helpful to categorize previous research into two main types: cross-sectional, correlational studies and experimental studies.

Cross-sectional, correlational studies

Perhaps the most obvious research approach is to look at associations between a measure of class size or pupil–teacher ratios on the one hand and measures of pupil attainment on the other. If we find that children's attainment tends to be better when they have been educated in smaller classes this would seem to suggest that smaller classes have helped. Unfortunately, research that has used this approach, even when large numbers of schools are involved, has tended to find little or no relationship, or, perversely, that pupils in larger classes do somewhat better than pupils in smaller classes. These results are obviously disconcerting because they seem so counter-intuitive. But the now well-understood problem with this kind of research, which looks at naturally occurring associations between size of class or PTRs and pupils' performance, is that we often do not know whether the results can be explained by another factor. It may be, for example, that poor attainers tend to be allocated to smaller classes, that more experienced teachers are given larger classes, or even that less experienced teachers are allocated smaller classes. There may, in other words, be another explanation for the results, other than the implausible conclusion that large classes are better for pupils.

The heart of the problem is that studies are difficult to interpret if they are confined to 'cross-sectional' or 'correlational' designs, that is, studies that are restricted to associations between factors, in this case class size and attainment, at the same point in time. It is better to set up longitudinal studies, within which account is taken of pupil differences at an earlier point, preferably at the start of school or at least the beginning of the year. These scores, and measures of other factors that might be expected to be implicated in any association between class size and attainment, can then be used in analysis, or controlled for, in order to examine the effect of class size on children's progress over a period of time. We need, therefore, more sophisticated types of design and analysis to control for other factors, in order to arrive at more definite conclusions about the effects of class size. I shall say more about how we approached our research design shortly.

We can include in this type of large-scale cross-sectional or correlational research a UK report from Ofsted (1995a). Given the very public way the conclusions were conveyed in the UK (*The Times* newspaper interpreted the study as showing that 'class size makes little difference'), and the way it was used by government ministers to support the view that class size is not important, it is helpful to look more closely at the methods used. This study was based on a large number of inspections by Ofsted inspectors in secondary schools in 1993/94 and primary schools in 1994/95. At the beginning of the report there is a disclaimer that inspectors working for Ofsted were not 'academic' researchers and because they were not specifically investigating the effects of class size, the results are therefore somehow more reliable. However, as Bassey (1996) has said, it is not the quantity of data, or how disinterested the researcher, that counts so much as the relevance of the questions asked and the research design and methods. In fact the Ofsted research is subject to the same problems of interpretation as other correlational research. In particular the cross-sectional design, for reasons given above, makes it impossible to provide a secure interpretation.

Given the way the results were interpreted it is interesting to note that in the report it states that at Key Stage 1 (which at this time included the Reception year) both the quality of learning and the quality of teaching were rated as better in smaller classes. Also lessons rated as 'less than sound' in terms of teaching and learning occurred less often in small classes. So, although much was made of how the results proved that class size had little effect, evidence was found for a link between class size and the quality of teaching and learning at KS1.

Experimental studies

It is often assumed that the problems of survey research are best overcome by the use of experimental research or randomized controlled trials. This is one reason for the great attention paid to the Tennessee STAR project, where in a bold and pioneering study the aim was to assign a large cohort of pupils and teachers at random to three types of classes within the same school: a small class (around 17 pupils), a regular class (around 23 students) and a regular class with a teacher aide. According to the logic of experimental designs, any later differences between groups must be attributable to the variable that has been experimentally manipulated, that is, to class size differences, and not to any other factor, for example, pre-existing differences between teachers or pupils. In brief, the researchers found that in both reading and maths, pupils in small classes performed significantly better than pupils in regular classes. Moreover, small classes with one qualified teacher had pupils who did better than pupils in regular classes with an assistant. Although findings are still contentious (see Mitchell et al. 1991; Prais 1996; Goldstein and Blatchford 1998; Grissmer 1999; Hanushek 1999), there is agreement that this is an impressive, large-scale study that provides evidence that smaller classes, at least below 20, have positive effects on pupil academic performance. It also shows that effects are most pronounced if introduced immediately after school entry, that is, with the youngest children in school (Finn and Achilles 1999; Nye et al. 2000). Reanalysis of the STAR data, using more sophisticated techniques, supported the central finding of a difference between small and regular classes (Goldstein and Blatchford 1998). It was also found that children from minority ethnic group backgrounds benefited most from small classes (Finn and Achilles 1999; Nye et al. 2000). In the experimental phase pupils were followed from kindergarten (aged 5) to third grade (aged 8). In fourth grade the pupils returned to regular classes and the experiment ended, but gains were still evident after a further three years, that is, grades 4–6 (Word et al. 1990; Nye et al. 1992).

The STAR project is a brilliant example of how education professionals, politicians and researchers can collaborate in a productive way. The professionals and politicians were convinced that small classes for young children were educationally valuable, but had the courage and tenacity to ask researchers to set up an objective study powerful enough to provide a reliable test of their conviction.

There is, then, no denying the power and importance of the STAR project, but there are some difficulties with the experimental research strategy that influenced our own choice of research design, as detailed below.

Generalizability

One of the big problems with experimental studies like the STAR project is that what they gain in control over the main variable of interest they can lose in the generalizability of results. One limitation is the narrow range of class sizes studied. What the STAR study compared, by UK standards at least, was very small classes of around 17 children with small classes of around 23. So we have no information on effects of class sizes outside this range. There are also difficulties in generalizing beyond the particular types of schools involved in the STAR project. The research design necessitated large three-form entry schools, but to what extent can we be sure that effects found in these schools will also be found in smaller schools, possibly with mixed aged classes?

Participants know they are in an experiment

Another difficulty, inherent in almost all experimental designs in educational settings, certainly in the STAR project, is that teachers and pupils in the study would have known which group they were in, that is, whether they were in a small or regular class. It is therefore difficult to know whether the results were due to class size differences as such or to another factor, for example, the expectations or resulting attitudes of those involved. It might be worth the reader putting themselves in the shoes of a teacher in the STAR project who had just been called to the head teacher's office on the first day of the school year to be told they had been assigned to a class with ten more children than a colleague who had just left from the same office. The news might be especially worrying if the school had a school inspection looming, or they had just read in the papers about the government's plans to introduce a performance-related pay scheme!

Financial and practical difficulties

There are also practical difficulties with experimental research on class size. If a main experimental condition involves class size reductions this probably entails employing more teachers, and can mean building costs to create extra classrooms. This can make the costs involved prohibitive.

Specific problems with STAR data

There are other difficulties with the STAR project in particular. It was found that there was considerable movement of pupils from year to year and the scores of those who dropped out of the study were lower than those who remained (Goldstein and Blatchford 1998). Although the children were assigned at random, the study would have been strengthened if there had been a baseline, that is, a school entry assessment measure, to thoroughly check that there were no prior differences between children in their academic attainments. Finally, the STAR project was not set up to examine *why* smaller classes were more effective on the basics, so we have little insight into the classroom processes involved.

General problems

The general problem with experimental designs is that they are inevitably difficult to interpret because they necessarily deviate from the 'real world' of education. Although there is an obvious point to the adage 'to understand something, change it', schools and education systems are complex and there are threats to validity if class size is studied in an artificial way, independent of the wider system. These points are not meant to imply that experimental designs cannot be of value, but it does mean that results have to be interpreted with more care than is sometimes the case. These kinds of worries about the validity of the experimental research, along with the practical difficulties in setting such a study up, made us decide on an alternative approach.

Features of the Institute of Education class size study: what makes it different?

It was our belief that it would be productive to research class size effects by seeking to capture the real and complex world of education rather than control one feature of it. It would, in other words, be more valid to seek better understanding of the effects of class size differences by measuring and examining relationships between class size and other factors, as they occur in the real world, and to make adjustments for possibly relevant factors such as children's prior attainments and family income. We felt that this design would offer a valuable source of evidence for policy because it would be more authentic. We could, for example, examine class size effects across the full range of class sizes, not just a few selected sizes. This could be important for policy recommendations, for example, if certain class sizes, or bands of class sizes, have stronger effects.

There were a number of key features to our research. These are summarized in Box 2.1.

Follow children from school entry

First, the age of the children involved was considered. In line with the STAR project's findings it seemed to us important to start from the moment children

Box 2.1 Institute of Education class size study: key features

1. Followed children from school entry
2. Followed children over time with a longitudinal design
3. Used sophisticated statistical modelling techniques
4. Careful study of classroom processes connected to class size differences
5. A multi-method approach.

entered school. Our study followed a large sample of children from school entry through the first three years of school, that is, children aged 4–7 years. This actually proved difficult because in many schools children enter throughout the school year rather than at one point; for example, they have termly and/or staggered entry to school. Though tempted to start in September at the beginning of Year 1, when all the children would have been in school – this would certainly have made our lives easier! – we decided to follow each child in the selected Reception classes from the moment of their entry into school.

Follow children over time with a longitudinal design

Second, for the reasons just given, we felt that there was a need to study pupils over time using a longitudinal design, and obtain measures of pupil attainment on entry to school. As we have seen, a probably unnecessary doubt has been cast on the STAR project because of the absence of baseline attainment data.

Use of sophisticated statistical modelling techniques

Third, it is important to use statistical methods that do justice to the complexity of educational systems, in which class size may have an effect. In particular it is important to build on recent advances in multilevel statistical analysis (see Goldstein 1995). The original statistical analysis used in the STAR research was rather simple in the sense that it did not take account of separate levels of child, class/teacher and school, all of which could have had an effect on results found. In our statistical analyses we used methods that would help us better estimate the real relationships between class size and pupils' achievement. These took account of the hierarchical structure of educational data, that is, that pupils are located within classes, which are located in schools, which are located in particular areas. We cannot assume that children are independent of the contexts within which they live and work. It is known that children in the same school class tend to be more alike, for example, in terms of their educational attainment levels, than children in different classes, children in the same school tend to be more alike than children in different schools, and so on. It has been shown that failure to take account of between-classroom and between-school sources of variation can adversely affect the accuracy of results (Goldstein 1995).

We also employed a more sophisticated approach to calculating the relationship between class size and achievement, than that conducted in previous research. Where a relationship has been found, a simple straight-line relationship is often assumed, though not tested. We felt that it was important to test this more precisely to see if the relationship, if it existed, was constant throughout the class size distribution. As class sizes increase are there certain points beyond which it begins to have a detrimental effect? Conversely do class sizes have to go lower than 20 for any appreciable effect to be noticed, as is often assumed? These types of questions have important policy implications but are answerable only if we examine relationships between different class sizes and achievement, that go beyond a simple test of their association. As we saw in Chapter 1, we also wanted to explore the separate effects of class size and the presence of teaching assistants in class to see whether extra support may be more important in larger classes.

We also wanted to establish whether class size and pupil–teacher ratio effects are modified in any way by characteristics of children, such as age, family income, gender, English as an additional language, previous preschool experiences and term of entry to school. This is important because research has suggested that smaller classes are more beneficial for some groups of children, for example, poor or minority groups (Finn and Achilles 1999; Molnar et al. 1999).

Another question we hoped to answer was whether the composition of the school class affected relationships between class size and children's progress. It is the experience of many teachers that it is not only class size that is important, but also the kinds of children in the class. So a class of just 15 children can be very difficult to teach if 5 of the children present emotional or behavioural difficulties (EBD) or find it hard to concentrate. A large class may be more manageable if a teacher has children who are already achieving well and are highly motivated. It might be expected that for a given size of class, a child will make more progress if the average ability level of the class is higher, and, conversely, less progress if there are more children who achieved poorly at pre-test, and have behavioural difficulties. Again, there was little information available to answer these questions.

Finally we needed to be sure that any relationships between class size and progress was not affected by teacher characteristics, such as teacher's experience, professional training and qualifications, and their perceived effectiveness.

Careful study of classroom processes connected to class size differences

Our study had a fourth feature. As I have argued, even if it can be shown that class size differences have an impact on pupils' academic progress, this still leaves unanswered questions about what mediates the effect. Research has concentrated almost exclusively on the effects of class size reductions on academic outcomes and we have little systematic information on what mediating processes might be involved. Finn and Achilles (1999: 102), two of the STAR research team, acknowledge this when they argue: 'Despite dozens of earlier studies, the classroom processes that distinguish small from large classes have proven elusive.' In a similar vein, Grissmer (1999) has concluded that there is a lack of coherent theories by which to guide and interpret empirical work on class size effects, and with which to make new predictions. The situation in the UK is much worse, in the sense that there is little research on classroom processes connected to class size differences. We need, therefore, information on classroom processes connected to class size differences, that might explain why smaller classes differ from larger classes.

It is not intended to provide a full review here of research on possible mediating factors (for reviews see Cooper 1989; Blatchford and Mortimore 1994; Day et al. 1996; Blatchford and Martin 1998; Anderson 2000). In the chapters that follow we describe the background to the classroom processes we studied. One main aim of the study was to develop an integrated model that would help describe connections between class size and classroom processes and attainment. This is presented in Chapter 9 of this book.

On the basis of a review of research and preparatory work, we identified the five classroom processes shown in Box 2.2 as most likely to mediate effects of class size differences.

A multi-method approach

The fifth main feature of the Institute of Education class size study stems from another limitation of previous research. One problem is the diversity of research methods used. Different research studies have used various research techniques including teacher report and interviews, questionnaires completed by teachers, teacher accounts of time spent, and observation studies, and it is not always clear whether they are covering the same phenomena. Integration of findings across studies is therefore made difficult. A more serious problem concerns the quality of research methods used in particular studies. Methods used are not always clearly described or adequate. Much is relatively anecdotal and based on teacher report and the reported experience of individual teachers. Though valuable, there are questions about the validity and generalizability of such views, especially given the fact that previous research has found discrepancies between teacher reports and classroom observation data

Box 2.2 Institute of Education class size study: classroom processes

1 Within-class groupings (for example the size and number of groups within the class)

Two processes connected to the teacher:

2 Teaching (for example teaching/instructional time versus organizational/ procedural time; amount of whole class, group and individual teaching; teaching, procedural, social and disciplinary interactions; other qualities of teaching interactions with children)
3 Individual support for reading

Two processes connected to the children:

4 Pupil inattentiveness
5 Peer relations

(Shapson et al. 1980). Large-scale secondary analyses (such as those in Betts and Shkolnik 1999; Rice 1999) are, in a technical sense, more reliable but have involved relatively crude, easily quantified, retrospective judgements of time allocation.

It seemed to us that an advance in understanding connections between class size and teaching would be to use a multi-method approach, in particular to integrate teachers' judgements and experiences with case studies, and also make use of carefully designed time allocation estimates as well as systematic observation data. As a general strategy it seemed to us important to consider different approaches not in opposition to each other but as complementary. There is also an acrimonious debate about different paradigms of educational research on teaching, with quantitative methods receiving much criticism (see Pellegrini and Blatchford 2000). Without wishing to gloss over the difficulties involved, there is much to be said for seeking to integrate different approaches, around a common frame of reference that would enable them to mutually inform each other.

In this research therefore we adopted a multiple method approach. We collected quantitative information that would enable us to address basic questions on relationships between class size and pupil–adult ratios, on the one hand, and teacher time allocation, teacher and pupil behaviour in class and children's school attainments, on the other hand. But we also wanted a more qualitative assessment of relationships between class size and teaching and individual support for reading, and understanding of the contribution of teaching assistants, through the use of methods that captured practitioners' experiences, and through detailed case studies. We have therefore deliberately sought to combine quantitative and qualitative approaches.

Schools, classes and children

Having explained the rationale and key features of the research I shall now describe the schools involved and the main types of information we collected.

The class size study followed for three years a large cohort of pupils who entered Reception classes (4–5 years) in English schools during 1996/97. (We also followed a second separate cohort of pupils who entered schools one year later, during 1997/98, though in this book we concentrate on results from cohort 1.) The children were followed for three years: Reception (4–5 years), Y1 (5–6 years) and Y2 (6–7 years).

Numbers of LEAs, schools, classes and pupils at the start of the study are shown in Table 2.1.

In the interests of anonymity, I shall not name the LEAs or the schools that took part in the study. I shall say, however, that although they involved more 'shire' than metropolitan authorities, they were a fairly representative sample, with rural and also inner city areas involved. The research design involved random selection of schools within the participating LEAs though of course schools were not compelled to take part, and we cannot rule out the possibility that those that did may have differed in some ways from those that did not. All children entering Reception classes in a selected school during the year were included in the study. The schools in the study drew from a wide range of social backgrounds, and were situated in urban, suburban and rural areas. At the start of the study there were almost equal numbers of boys and girls. About 17 per cent were eligible for free school meals (a measure of low family income), which was about the same as in England more generally. The vast majority (97 per cent) spoke English as a first language, and most (91 per cent) were classified as from white UK ethnic backgrounds. Schools were either all through primary schools (that is, children aged 4–11 years: 74 per cent) or infant schools (that is, children aged 4–7 years: 26 per cent).

Table 2.1 Numbers of LEAs, schools, classes and pupils at the start of the study

Number of LEAs	9
Number of schools	199
Number of classes	330
Number of pupils	7142

Types of data collected

In line with the multi-method approach described above there were a number of forms of data collected in the study, as shown in Box 2.3. Each of these forms of data collection will be described briefly.

Box 2.3 Types of data collected

- Pupil start of school and end of year attainments
- Information on children, classes and teachers
- Within-class groupings
- Teacher end of year questionnaires
- Case studies of selected classes
- Teacher estimates of time allocation
- Systematic classroom observations
- Pupil behaviour ratings

Pupil start of school and end of year attainments

School entry attainment

Information was collected when pupils entered school by means of a baseline entry assessment conducted by the teacher (LEA Class Size Research Project 1996). We adapted the Avon Reception Entry Assessment (1996), which we felt, after much searching, was one of the best schemes then available. It covered literacy and mathematics and comprised information not only from teacher ratings, based on classroom observations, but also from tasks completed by children. A measure of literacy knowledge was derived by adding for each child scores on 15 items in language, 18 in reading, 17 in writing and a test of letter identification (how many of 26 letters were recognized in terms of either name or sound). A measure of early mathematical concepts was based on total correct out of 19 items. Training was provided for class teachers by staff who had been involved in the design of the Avon scheme.

End of Reception year assessments

At the end of the Reception year, the Literacy Baseline component of the *Reading Progress Test* (Vincent et al. 2000) was administered by teachers. It reflected well the literacy curriculum experienced by children in English schools at the time. In the case of mathematics, a teacher-administered test was devised and extensively piloted. Again it reflected well the curriculum experienced by children of this age. The final version covered counting, repeating patterns, comparison and matching, addition using pictures, subtraction using pictures, addition and subtraction using words, addition and subtraction using symbols, and shape recognition.

End of Year 1 and Year 2 assessments

At the end of Year 1 the children were given the Young's group reading and mathematics tests, and at the end of Year 2 government-set standard assessment tasks (SATs) were coded using a specially adapted protocol, which captured raw scores on a continuous scale (rather than the restricted range of levels used by the government and schools when reporting results, which are of limited value for research purposes).

Connections between class size and these attainment measures are described in Chapter 8.

Information on children, classes and teachers

Information was collected for each child on term of entry, free school meal eligibility, age, ethnic background, preschool attendance, English as an additional language, special needs status, and gender. Information was collected on classes in the study in terms of class sizes (as on the school register, and also in terms of the number of children in the class at a given point in the term – called 'experienced' class size), and on adults present, using three categories: whether they were teachers, staff other than teachers, and other adults (including, and mainly, parents). Details were also collected on the age mix of the class and classroom size in square metres. Information on teachers in the study was collected from self-completed questionnaires and comprised: teacher age, number of years of teaching experience, number of years in the current school, non-contact time, professional training and a rating of head teachers concerning their abilities as teachers.

A full list of child, class and teacher variables used in the statistical analyses is shown in Table 8.1.

Within-class groupings

Quantitative data

We wanted to get a description of grouping practices within classes that captured in a standardized way some basic features that we could use in numerical analysis. The method we designed combined the benefits of a large-scale survey method, and a more detailed observational approach. It was developed by my colleague Peter Kutnick and myself some years ago in the course of a series of studies we have co-directed on within-class grouping practices. Teachers, at a given time in the school day when pupils were working (as opposed to break time or assembly), drew a map of their classroom. On this map they identified the location of individual male and female pupils, the grouping that they were part of, and adults working in the classroom. Later, at a convenient moment, teachers completed a short questionnaire on each grouping giving information on the size of the group, composition of the group in terms of its ability level and whether it was comprised of friends, whether adults were with the group, the type of interaction between children (for example whether working alone but on the same task, or working together to produce an end product), and the curriculum area and type of task being worked on. Information was also collected on the size of the class at the time of the mapping survey.

The quantitative results were based on two connected studies. First, data were drawn from the termly questionnaires completed by Reception class teachers in the class size study (these are described shortly). Data came from 485 classes and resulted in information on 2094 groupings. In addition, and in order to extend the coverage of ages and increase the sample size, data were also used from a separate but connected project funded by the Economic and Social Research Council. This was the Primary Grouping Practices Project (PGPP) and it was co-directed by Peter Kutnick and myself. Five LEAs (different from those in the class size study) were involved, four from the south and one from the north-west of England. Three were mostly urban and two inner city. Participating schools were sent grouping mapping questionnaires to be completed by Year 2 and Year 5 teachers during a week when extraneous events, which may have made groupings untypical, were not timetabled. A total of 425 schools were contacted and just under half agreed to assist with the project. Over half of these schools returned questionnaires. A total of 1063 groupings in total were described in the questionnaires of the 187 Year 2 and Year 5 classes. Although the data from Year 5 classes fall outside the focus in this book on Reception and KS1, the results for the three years were analysed together and I have included them all here to convey the full picture over the whole of the primary stage.

Taking the data on classroom groups from the two studies together (that is, the PGPP and class size studies) therefore resulted in 672 classes in 311 schools, and a database comprising 3157 groupings in all. More details on the methods used can be found in Blatchford et al. (1999, 2001a) and Kutnick et al. (2002).

Qualitative data

In order to complement the numerical results on grouping within classes, we also collected more open-ended interpretative information on groups. There were two sources of qualitative data:

- In the second stage of the PGPP, case studies were conducted in twelve Year 2 and Year 5 classrooms (six at each level) from eight schools – two junior (7–11 years) and six primary schools (4–11 years). Teachers of these classes had returned questionnaires and were selected to provide a range of classroom layouts. Part of these case studies involved semistructured interviews with teachers, which were shaped around a number of key areas (see Blatchford et al. (1999) for more details on the methodology). Only results from the interviews concerning Year 2 classes are used here.

- Questionnaires completed by class teachers at the end of each school year included a general question asking about class size experiences over the year in relation to teaching and learning. Responses were analysed in terms of a coding frame developed during pilot work. Quotes from interviews and questionnaires were selected to be representative, and to complement the numerical results.

Data on within-class groupings are presented in Chapter 3.

Teacher end of year questionnaires

One main source of information in the study was from questionnaires sent out near the end of each school year in which we asked teachers about their experiences and views on selected topics. For the purposes of this analysis we analysed questionnaires completed by 151 Reception teachers (cohort 2), 208 Year 1 teachers (cohort 1), 130 Year 1 teachers (cohort 2) and 153 Year 2 teachers (cohort 1). The aim was to describe teachers' views and experiences in a thorough way by collecting information from a substantial number each year during Reception and Key Stage 1, and by a careful analysis of the range and types of answers given. The analysis combined quantitative analysis of the prevalence of different categories of answers with illustrative and verbatim quotations from teachers' written answers.

For this book, answers to two questions from the questionnaire were used. One concerned whether, and in what ways, teachers felt that class size differences had affected teaching and learning over the year, and the other asked for teachers' views on the contribution of other staff and adults in the classroom. Questions were open-ended, with space provided for comments. A coding frame was developed on the basis of an initial analysis of 70 questionnaires. Answers were read through, and categories were devised which captured the most frequent themes. Different members of the research team worked on the same corpus of teachers' responses and periodically categories were checked in terms of reliability and validity. The remainder of the questionnaires were then read through, and all teachers' answers were categorized in terms of the system developed earlier. Categories coded for each teacher were entered for statistical analysis. More than one category could be entered for each teacher. The questionnaires were completed by all teachers in the study, whatever the number of children in the class. Some comments were therefore about experiences of large classes, while some might refer to the same point (for example, regarding individual attention) from the point of view of small classes. These are discussed together under the appropriate category.

Data from this analysis are used for the sections on the effect of class size on teaching (Chapter 4), the effect of class size on individual reading support (Chapter 5) and the role of teaching assistants in classes (Chapter 7).

Case studies of selected classes

Case studies were conducted to provide complementary information to that in other quantitative components of the study. The aim was to provide a more detailed portrayal of individual classes, which would provide the basis for a more interpretive and grounded analysis of factors relating to staff and adult deployment in class. Schools were selected with differing class size categories: large (30 and over), large medium (26–29), small medium (20–25) and small (under 20). The aim was to study two classes in each class size band in each year (Reception, Year 1 and Year 2), totalling 24 classes in all. Procedures differed for the Reception year because classes are more likely to see changes over the year (for example because of termly entry). Visits to the eight classes took place each term. For Years 1 and 2, there were three visits in the spring term.

The methodology was developed on the basis of field visits to schools. Selected aspects of classroom learning and experience, expected to be connected to class size differences, were defined in advance, and then on the basis of field visits were refined into the following main headings:

- physical space
- grouping practices
- establishment of routines
- classroom discipline
- tasks and curriculum
- teacher–pupil interactions and knowledge of children
- teacher stress and enthusiasm
- atmosphere/ethos
- assessments and record keeping
- pupil adjustment and peer relations
- relationships with parents
- special educational needs (SEN).

In this book we use the information from case studies in the chapters on teaching factors connected to class size, children's concentration in class, and the deployment of non-teaching staff.

The method used in case studies comprised the following components:

1 Event sampling of significant events

- *Whole class observations:* continuous notes were made of the activities of the whole class, and groups working at the time. Observers noted on the sheets the time every five minutes but times of changes in activities were also noted, for example when a group of children moved to another task. The nature of the task and curriculum area, and the nature of the interactions between teachers, other adults, and children were described.
- *Child focus observations:* three children in each class were observed (one high, one medium and one low ability). Again the main headings were used, as in the main observations above, to organize observation notes. As before, times were noted. The aim was to obtain more insight into children's adjustment to school, in terms of the above headings.

2 Semistructured interviews with teachers and the head teacher, organized in terms of the main headings above.
3 End of session/day comments and judgements by fieldworkers in terms of main headings, related to class size differences.
4 Summative judgements by fieldworkers in terms of the main headings, and end of year discussion between research team and fieldworkers.

This component made use of experienced teachers as fieldworkers. Quite deliberately, the aim in this component was to marry aspects of systematic observation (which emphasized the objectivity of data), with professional and interpretative judgements by experienced teachers

Data from the case studies are used in Chapters 4, 5 and 7.

Teacher estimates of time allocation

These included overall teaching time, teaching individuals, groups or the whole class, and reading activities.

Teaching time allocation

Data came from the termly questionnaires completed by class teachers. They were given a pre-selected set of activities and asked for a given half-day session to estimate the time in minutes spent on each activity. The activities were selected on the basis of pilot work, and were grouped into two broad types. First, teaching activities:

- teaching/working with the whole class
- working with an individual child
- working with a group of children.

Second, aspects of classroom management and other non-teaching activities:

- collecting dinner money
- liaising with other adults in the classroom
- dealing with domestic and personal problems such as toileting, accidents, and so on
- outside interruptions such as telephone calls, receiving visitors, and so on
- lining the class up, putting on coats, and so on
- time out of class
- taking the register
- settling the class and allocating tasks and children to groups
- dealing with discipline and behaviour problems.

The three teaching activity categories – time in minutes teaching to individuals, groups and the whole class – were used separately and also added to give an estimate of the total time in minutes in teaching activities. The totals in minutes were then converted to percentages of the session time (because in some classes the session may have been reduced by times out of the class and unexpected events). There were then four measures for each teacher:

- percentage time teaching individuals
- percentage time teaching groups
- percentage time teaching the whole class
- total percentage time in teaching (that is, the sum of the above three categories).

In this book, only termly questionnaire data from cohort 1 was used. Data came from teachers of 279 Reception classes, 207 Year 1 classes and 118 Year 2 classes.

It is recognized that some 'non-teaching' activities can be sometimes considered teaching activities, but it was felt that adding the three teaching modes – which asked the teacher specifically about teaching – would provide the most unambiguous estimate of time spent by the teacher in teaching.

These data are used in Chapters 4 and 7.

Reading activities in class

Teachers were also asked for information on time spent in a number of reading activities in class. This book reports on teachers' estimates of two types of activities:

- frequency of reading aloud to an adult in school, in terms of four categories: daily, three or four times a week, once or twice a week, less than weekly
- duration of time each child was heard read by an adult per week this term, in terms of four categories: less than 5 minutes, 6–10 minutes, 11–20 minutes, more than 20 minutes.

These data are used in Chapter 5.

Systematic classroom observations

Because of the labour-intensive nature of systematic observation data, and because the first year of school was of particular interest, the observation component reported in this book involved a subsample of Reception classes (children aged 4–5 years). Three of the participating LEAs were approached and agreed to take part in the observation component. Schools were selected on the basis of information already provided on class sizes. Schools with small (20 or fewer) and large (30 and over) Reception classes were identified and a random selection approached to see if they were willing to take part. The aim was to get 40 classes, divided between large and small classes. In the event 39 classes in 27 schools with the required characteristics agreed to take part. There were 18 large and 21 small classes. Those identified as small classes had on average 19.4 children and those identified as large classes had on average 32.5 children. For each class, observers were provided with the names of 6 children randomly chosen by the researchers along with 2 reserves to be observed in cases where the sample children were absent. In the event there were observations on 235 children (one class had observations on 7 children).

A systematic observation schedule developed in previous research (Blatchford et al. 1987; Tizard et al. 1988) was used. This involved direct (on the spot) observations of selected children in terms of previously developed categories. The schedule was child based in the sense that one child at a time was observed, the 'target' child. The aim was to provide a description of the child's behaviour; teachers and other children were observed only if they came into contact with the target when he or she was being observed. The basic categories contained in the schedule are shown in Figure 2.1. At any moment in time a child could be in one of three 'social modes' – they could be interacting with their teachers, with other children or not interacting. Within each of these three 'modes' a child's behaviour could be task/work related, procedural/managerial, social/personal or off-task.

Target children were observed in terms of 5-minute observation sheets divided into continuous 10-second time samples. The basic principle was to observe during classroom-based work activities, that is, those parts of the day

	Social 'mode'		
Type of behaviour	*Teacher–child*	*Child–child*	*Not interacting*
Task related			
Procedural/managerial			
Social/personal			
Off-task			

Figure 2.1 Systematic observation: basic categories

when language, maths, other work like craft and painting, and free play in the classroom could have taken place. The aim was to observe the six children in each class five times per day, for three days. In the event there were on average 413 observations (that is, 10-second time interval observations) per child. This amounted to nearly 100,000 observations overall! Observers were recently retired senior teachers and head teachers, contacted through participating LEAs, who then received initial training, practice observations in a Reception class not involved in the study, and then a follow-up training session. Reliability checks (that is, the extent to which independent observers agreed on the occurrence of behaviours) were carried out through the training sessions. A reliability study carried out in earlier work showed that observer agreement was high.

There is not space to provide full definitions and conventions of categories (see Blatchford et al. 1987; Tizard et al. 1988; Blatchford 2002). Main categories, with brief definitions, were as follows.

Teacher–child contact

1. *Social setting:* one-to-one, group or whole class.
2. *Child role: focus* (target child is focus of teacher's attention) or *audience* (another child is focus in group or class involving target child, or teacher interacts to same extent with all children). These two sets of categories described the behaviour coded in the 'teacher content' section.
3. *Teacher content: task-teach:* contacts directly concerned with the substantive content of children's task activities, by communicating concepts, facts or ideas by explaining, informing, demonstrating, questioning, suggesting ('task' here includes any activity in settings, other than transition times). *Task-preparation:* contacts directly

concerning the organization and preparation of children's task activities and not their substantive content. *Task-silent:* a teacher's contribution to task contact is passive, such as hearing child read, looking over child's work. *Procedure:* contacts concerned with classroom management and organization of classroom routine, often at transition times, such as milk, washing, changing, organizing materials. *Social:* personal or social comments, for example about life outside the classroom, children's appearance, health, and so on. *Unclear:* not possible to code reliably.

Child–teacher contact

1. *Child contribution:* child's contribution to interaction with teacher in terms of *respond* to teacher, *initiate* contact with teacher, *attend* to teacher, *continued* interaction from previous time intervals and *unclear*. These categories describe the child's contribution to the behaviour coded in the 'child content' section. If the child interacted in an overt way ('respond', 'initiate', 'continued'), these were coded; only when the child attended for the whole 10-second interval was 'attend' coded. Because of its likely low frequency of occurrence, 'initiate' was given priority over 'respond' if both occurred within the same interval. Predominant activity sampling therefore (see below) was not used for the 'child contribution' categories.
2. *Child content: task:* all child behaviours in contact with teacher that are concerned with 'task' as defined for 'teacher content' (above). *Procedure:* equivalent to teacher 'procedure' (above). *Social:* equivalent to teacher 'social' (above). *Inappropriate:* child behaviour to teacher obviously unrelated to teacher request or situation, such as not answering a question on maths, but making a comment about a television programme the previous evening. *Off-task:* child behaviour involving the teacher, but not directed at the teacher, that is, inappropriate or unrelated to situation (for example not attending to story). *Unclear:* not possible to code reliably (as above).

Child–child contact

Coded when child is in contact with other children but not teacher. *Task:* all contacts with other children that are concerned with the content of 'tasks' as defined for 'teacher content' (above). *Procedure:* all contacts with other children concerning classroom organization and routine. *Social:* social or personal contacts not related to work or procedure. *Mucking about:* contacts that involve fooling around. Like social contacts, they are not about task or procedural activities, but are more obviously off-task. *Aggressive:* target child is aggressive (verbally or physically) towards other child(ren). *Help:* target child helps another child, such as helping to tie their shoelaces. *Unclear:* behaviour with other children that cannot be coded reliably (as above).

Not interacting

Coded during time intervals when child is not in contact with teacher or other children. *Task-involved:* target child is involved in own 'task' activity (as defined for 'teacher content', above). *Procedure:* activity concerned with procedure or routine. *Off-task (active):* target child focuses on something other than task in hand. *Off-task (passive):* target child is disengaged during task activity, such as wandering around or daydreaming. *Audience:* target child observes other children or teacher when not in contact with them. *Unclear:* behaviour when not interacting that cannot be reliably coded (as above).

The systematic observation data are used in Chapters 4 and 6.

Pupil behaviour ratings (PBR)

As described in Chapter 6, we felt that existing ways of measuring pupils' attentiveness and peer relations were not satisfactory for our purposes, first, on conceptual grounds, in terms of how different aspects of social and behaviour aspects of school behaviour were defined, second, because of technical concerns, in terms of the structure of the measures and the reliability of subscales, and third, because of their length and their appropriateness for the age of children in our study.

Given the numbers of pupils involved in the project, and the way that teachers have privileged information about children in their class, we decided that a teacher-administered procedure would be preferable. Teachers are likely to be more knowledgeable than observers with regard to such dimensions. We also required an efficient measure that teachers, given their other commitments to the research project, would not find inconvenient and too time consuming to complete.

The pupil behaviour rating (PBR) was developed at the Institute of Education for the class size study. It drew from other behaviour rating scales (particularly Ladd and Profilet's (1996) *Child Behavior Scale*, with additional items taken from Thompson's (1975) Adjustment to School Scale, Rowe's (1995) Behavioural Rating Inventory, the LEA Class Size Research Project (1996), and the *Pre-School Behaviour Checklist* (McGuire and Richman 1988).

Teachers completed a PBR for every child in the study. In this book data from cohort 1 are used. The PBR comprised over 50 items rated on a three-point scale ('certainly applies to this child', 'applies sometimes to this child', 'does not apply to this child'). Scores on conceptually and empirically linked items that made up a set of factors were added. The reliability of these scales was high. The six factors were:

- inattentive-distractible (15 items)
- anxious-fearful (4 items)
- aggressive with peers (14 items)
- asocial with peers (6 items)
- excluded by peers (7 items)
- prosocial with peers (7 items).

Information from the PBR scales is used in Chapter 6.

Having explained the background to the design of the research, and described the types of information we collected, I shall discuss the first results to be presented in this book – on within-class groups – in the next chapter.

3 Connections between class size and within-class grouping

We have seen that research on the effects of class size differences needs not only to look at relations with academic outcomes, but also to provide insights into classroom processes that might explain why smaller classes differ from large classes.

In Chapter 1 I argued that research on teaching and classroom processes has tended to assume an underlying direct model, in the sense that the focus has been on the effect of teachers on pupils' attainments, while in fact teachers (and pupils) will necessarily need to adapt to the classroom context, which will include features such as the number of children in the class. But there are also contexts nested *within* classrooms. Before we examine links between class size differences and teacher and pupil behaviour, we first need to explore the connections between class size and one main within-class context, namely groupings within the class.

All pupils in classes are grouped in some form or another, perhaps especially at primary school level in Britain, and the group is a main context for teaching and learning. Let us take an example of a small class of 20 pupils. Here a teacher may have children seated in groups of 5 around four tables. If the teacher has given out the same worksheet to all children there will be four groupings. If later in the lesson the teacher then goes over the worksheet with the children as a class, there will be only one grouping; even though children are seated at four tables their attention and activity is focused on the teacher and the rest of the class as a whole. This example illustrates that a grouping at any moment in time may be an individual child, a pair (dyad), triad, or anything from a small group of four children to a whole class grouping.

The benefits or disadvantages of different grouping practices has aroused a good deal of comment and research in Britain and elsewhere. In Britain, 'progressive' primary education practices, including small group work, have been criticized as being ineffective (Alexander et al. 1992; Ofsted 1995b), and it has been recommended that teachers adopt whole class teaching methods, albeit tempered with a recognition that pupils need to be interactive rather than passive. Recent government curriculum strategies (such as the commonly called 'literacy hour') are prescriptive about time to be spent in particular groupings. Even when group work is recommended, the assumption is that it will be led by the teacher.

However, a number of researchers have produced studies that indicate a more positive role for within-class groups. Lou et al. (1996) showed the advantages of small group instruction in terms of peer learning, flexibility over learning objectives and meeting individual needs, and encouragement of higher-order learning skills. Experimental research also paints a more positive picture (Johnson and Johnson 1987), although such studies are difficult to interpret in the sense that they may not reflect the range of groupings that occur under everyday conditions in classrooms. In fact, surprisingly little is known about within-class grouping in terms of a number of key dimensions, including the size and number of groups in a class.

The class and the group can be thought of as different environmental contexts, with the group level nested within the level of the whole class. Logically the two levels, that is class size and within-class groups, *have* to be connected. As class size increases groups must either become bigger or more numerous. If, in the above example, the teacher was faced with a class of 32, rather than one of 20, then she could divide her class into four groupings of 8 pupils, eight groupings of 4 pupils, or a range of different sized groupings, or teach the class as a whole in one large grouping. In each case the number of groups or the size of groups increases. But the conceptual, and educationally important, question concerns *how*, in practice, class size and within-class groupings are connected. As far as I know, this possibility, that is, the connection between size of class and within-class grouping practices, has not been looked at systematically before.

Within-class groups: core themes

In this chapter I draw on ideas from a programme of research on within-class groups that I have co-directed with Peter Kutnick. I introduced this research in Chapter 2. In this research we have provided a systematic and multi-dimensional description of within-class groups in primary schools (and in secondary schools – though these results are not discussed in this book). We also developed a novel method of obtaining information on groups – through a classroom map drawn by the teacher at an allotted time in the school day – and this is described in Chapter 2. In our research, within-class groupings were conceptualized and measured in terms of several 'core themes'. This chapter draws on results from this research, as well as from the class size study (as explained in Chapter 2), and is concerned with connections between class size and three of these themes: the size and number of groups in the class, the role of teachers in pupil groups, and the type of interaction between children in the groups. (Interested readers can find more on our research on primary school groups in Blatchford et al. 1999; Kutnick et al. 2002 and on secondary school groups in Blatchford et al. 2001a.)

Size and number of groups in the class

Research on grouping has been mostly concerned with the composition of groups, usually in terms of ability (Lou et al. 1996; Webb et al. 1997). However, another basic component, that is likely to affect a pupil's educational experience, is not only the size of the group they work in, but also the number of groups in a class. We felt that research to date had not looked in a systematic way at the range of group sizes as they naturally occur in classrooms, and at the connections with activities and interactions in these groups.

A large class is likely to present teachers with some difficult choices. One strategy might be to use more whole class teaching, that is, to treat the whole class as one group. In every class there will be a need for whole class teaching sessions, and in some countries there is a strong tradition of whole class teaching. But certainly in the UK, during the primary school years, there will also be times, and in the case of certain activities, when this is not appropriate. There will also be difficulties with whole class teaching when the class contains children of diverse aptitudes, or with very young children. In larger classes teachers may then be forced to organize the class into, and teach more to, larger groups than they would like. In a small class, by contrast, there may be more opportunity for individualized or very small group work, and more individual attention. As Lou et al. (1996) show, whole class and small group contexts are likely to have very different pedagogical consequences, with whole class teaching having more emphasis on teacher explanations and encouragement and uniformity of instruction, and small group instruction likely to involve more peer interaction and diverse learning activities. A main aim of this chapter is therefore to investigate the links between class size and number and size of groups, as well as teachers' experience of, and views on, the connections.

Role of teachers in pupil groups

The role of teachers with regard to groups is likely to be crucial, practically in their effective management of classrooms, and also in terms of connections with other aspects of group functioning. There is however little systematic information available on how teachers distribute their time between groups within the class, and whether this varies between groups of different size. It might be expected that the number of children in the class will necessarily have implications for the amount and quality of contact that teachers can offer separate groups.

Type of interaction between children in the groups

Another key feature is the nature of the interaction between pupils. One criticism of the use of groupings in schools is that although children often sit and work in groups it is rare that they work *as* groups (Galton et al. 1980; Tizard et al. 1988). In this chapter a categorization of interaction within groupings (Bennett and Dunne 1992), which aimed to examine the working relationships between pupils, was extended to incorporate pupil–teacher interactions. The aim was to find out whether children tend to work more collaboratively in smaller groups and classes as might be expected.

Results

In this chapter I shall, therefore, examine the links between class size and within-class groups in terms of three core themes: number and size of groups in the class, the role of teachers in pupil groups, and the type of interaction between children in the groups. I do this on the basis of quantitative analyses of more than 3000 groupings and complementary qualitative analyses of interviews and questionnaires from teachers.

Class size in relation to number of groups in the class

As I described in Chapter 2, we asked teachers at an allotted time in the school day to draw a map of the location of each child and the groups they were in. They then provided information on each group relating to the three core themes. Looking first at the number of groups in the class at the time, Table 3.1 shows that there were on average just under five groups at the time of the classroom map. (For the sake of completion I have included results on children in Year 5, even though they are older than those described in the rest of the book.) The number of groups in classes increased significantly with the age of child between Reception, Year 2 and Year 5 (4.4, 5.3 and 6.1 on average respectively), so the older children were in classes with more groups. This trend was statistically significant. (Here, and in the rest of the book, in order not to interrupt the text, and in the interests of the non-technical reader, I have not given full details of statistical analyses. Those interested will find the full details in the papers referred to in the text and in the References.)

In this chapter and others I shall look at class size in two main ways: as a 'continuous variable', in terms of the actual numbers of children in the class, and as a 'categorical variable', that is class size divided into four

Table 3.1 Average number of groups by registered class size and year group

	Year group							
	Reception		*Year 2*		*Year 5*		*Total*	
Registered class size	*Average*	*n*	*Average*	*n*	*Average*	*n*	*Average*	*n*
10–20	3.2	66	4	6	3.4	7	3.3	79
21–25	3.9	120	5.2	18	6.2	25	4.4	163
26–30	4.6	209	5.3	41	6.4	44	5.0	294
31+	5.4	89	5.9	25	6.4	19	5.6	133
Total	4.4	484	5.3	90	6.1	95	4.7	669

groups: 10–20, 21–25, 26–30, or more than 30. Classes of fewer than 20 might be seen, in the UK context anyway, as 'small' and classes of more than 30, as 'large'.

Table 3.1 also shows that the number of groups in a class increased with the size of the class, and this was evident whether class size was treated as a continuous or categorical variable. The effect was evident at all three ages. Looking at the last set of columns headed 'Total' it can be seen that over all three year groups, small classes (that is, 20 children or fewer) had on average just over three groups, while in large classes there were approaching six groups.

Class size in relation to size of groups in the class

Let us now turn to the size of the groups in classes. In Table 3.2, the average size of grouping across all three age levels is seen to be just over five children (this is shown in the last set of columns again labelled 'Total'). Group sizes varied by age of child; groups in classes with older children (Year 5) were significantly smaller than those in Year 2 and Reception classes. This means that the youngest children in school tend to be in the largest groups but the least number of groups.

The connections between size of class and the size of within-class groups are also shown in Table 3.2 overall and for the three year groups separately. Overall, the size of groups in the class decreased with size of class, from 5.4 in large classes and 4.6 in small classes. Looking at the three year groups separately, Table 3.2 also shows that the association between class size and size of groups was found at Reception and at Year 5. At Year 2, the average size of groups increases with size of class bands in the expected fashion, though the differences were not statistically significant.

Table 3.2 Average size of groups by registered class size and year group

Registered class size	*Group size*			
	Reception	*Year 2*	*Year 5*	*Total*
10–20	4.8	4.7	3.4	4.6
21–25	5.6	4.6	3.8	5.1
26–30	5.7	5.2	4.3	5.4
31+	5.6	5.5	4.8	5.4
Total	5.6	5.1	4.2	5.3

The connection between class size and group size can be examined in more detail by looking at the relationship between the four class size categories, as already described, and group size categorized into the following bands: individuals, dyads, triads, 4–6s, 7–10s, and 11+. This was done on conceptual grounds, based on previous research (Kutnick 1994), and was also consistent with the distribution of group sizes. These results are shown in Table 3.3.

Looking first just at the size of group, it can be seen that a pupil is most likely to experience a group size of 4–6 children – about half of all groups were of this size – followed by larger groups of 7–10 and 11 or more children (mostly whole classes). Turning to the association between class size and group size, the main trend evident in Table 3.3 is that in class sizes over 25 there is more likelihood of a pupil being in a large group of 7–10, while in classes under 25 there is more likelihood of being in a very large group of 11 and over. There is relatively little likelihood of children in classes under 25 being in groups of 7–10. We can also see in Table 3.3 a slight tendency for more smaller groups,

Table 3.3 Connections between registered class size and group size (both treated as categorical variables)

Registered class size	*Group size as a category*						
	Individuals (%)	*Dyads (%)*	*Triads (%)*	*4–6s (%)*	*7–10s (%)*	*11+ (%)*	*Total (%)*
10–20	1.8	8.3	8.8	48.9	6.3	26.0	7
21–25	1.5	6.6	6.4	50.2	9.3	25.9	22
26–30	1.0	4.8	4.3	50.2	24.3	15.4	46
31+	1.2	5.1	5.3	44.6	25.8	18.0	24
Total	1.2	5.5	5.4	48.7	20.1	19.1	

particularly dyads and triads, in smaller classes. The results shown in Table 3.3 are for all three year groups added together. The relationship between class size and size of group was also conducted at each age level. The effect just described was clearest at Reception level.

Role of teachers in pupil groups

In general, teachers were most likely to be present in groups in Reception classes (48 per cent of groupings), followed by Year 2 classes (26 per cent of groupings). Groupings in Year 5 classes were the least likely to have an adult present (16 per cent).

There was also a significant relationship between adult presence and group size at all three ages. As might be expected, teachers were most likely to be with the largest groups – 7–10s and especially 11+ groups (which included whole classes). But adults were also more likely to be working with individuals than with dyads, triads and 4–6 children. At all ages, dyads and triads were *least* likely to have teachers present.

Type of interaction between children in the groups

There were four types of categories: working alone, working alone but on the same task as the group, working together to produce a group product and interacting with the teacher and the rest of the class or group. The relationship between type of interaction, categorized in this way, and group size, again divided into whether they were individuals, dyads, triads 4–6s, 7–10s or 11 or more, is shown in Table 3.4.

It can be seen that the most common type of interaction between group members was actually no interaction at all. In about two-thirds of all groupings children were engaged in individual work that did not require interaction among group members. There were far fewer groupings – 12 per cent – in which children were working together in a cooperative way to produce a group product. Finally, approximately one-fifth of groupings involved pupils listening to and interacting with the teacher and the rest of the class or group.

Turning now to the connection between type of interaction and group size, Table 3.4 also shows that working together was more likely in smaller groups (dyads, triads and to an extent groups of 4–6 children), and much less likely in large groups of 7–10 children.

The final table in this chapter – Table 3.5 – shows the connection between class size and type of interaction. Consistent with the results on group size in relation to size of class, it was also found that children in smaller classes were relatively more likely to interact with the teacher and the rest of the class or group. Individual work, that is, working alone but in a group, to a degree increases with size of class. Interestingly, working together to produce a group

Table 3.4 Proportion of different sized groupings that participated in different types of interactions and working arrangements (Years 2 and 5 only)

	Type of interaction				
Group size	*Working alone (%)*	*Working alone but on the same task as group (%)*	*Working together to produce a group product (%)*	*Interacting with teacher and rest of class/group (%)*	*Total (%)*
Individuals	33	67*	–	–	10
Dyads	–	76	24	1	23
Triads	–	67	31	3	11
4–6s	–	81	14	5	46
7–10s	–	79	6	15	7
11+	–	10	0	90	4
Total	0.7	63.4	12.2	23.8	100

Note: * These individuals were working on a task that was also being undertaken by other children seated at another table.

Table 3.5 Connections between registered class size and different types of interactions and working arrangements (Years 2 and 5 only)

	Type of interaction				
Registered class size	*Working alone (%)*	*Working alone but on the same task as group (%)*	*Working together to produce a group product (%)*	*Interacting with teacher and rest of class/group (%)*	*Total (%)*
10–20	1.3	55.7	4.8	38.2	4.7
21–25	0.5	61.0	12.8	25.7	20.2
26–30	0.8	62.4	15.3	21.5	46.0
31+	0.5	67.7	8.0	23.8	29.0
Total	0.7	63.4	12.2	23.8	

product (cooperative or collaborative group work), although not common, as we have seen, was *less* likely in small, and to an extent, large classes, and more likely in classes with between 20 and 30 children. Our expectation that we would find more cooperative group work in smaller classes was therefore not confirmed.

Qualitative analyses

One of the main points to emerge from the qualitative study concerned difficulties larger classes placed on teachers in terms of grouping arrangements. A main difficulty faced by teachers was what might be called a 'size/number dilemma'. This is evident in the following extract from a Year 2 teacher:

> When I first had this class I had 33 children in it and I tried to group them into five groups but I just didn't have enough space and so then I had to put them into four groups of eight and they were a bit unwieldy. Eight is rather too many and now that some have left it's a much better arrangement – five groups of six because the tables are not so bulky and the children are more separated from each other away from the other groups and six is a smaller number to work with – it's a manageable number to work with, so I would definitely say that [class size] is quite a definite factor.
>
> (Year 2 teacher)

It is evident here that the number of children created difficulties for the teacher, in terms of organizing the class, and she felt that a reduction in class size resolved the dilemma. There was a clear indication that teachers of large classes felt driven, for classroom management purposes, to use a few large groups rather than a number of small groups.

Group size preference

Teachers also commented on the relationship between the size of class and the size of the group. Some said that group size depended on the activity but the majority preferred group sizes of between four and six children for most purposes, including the lack of resources for larger groups, space restrictions, and the forced formality of larger groups.

Effects on teaching and learning of larger groups

The quantitative results showed the greater likelihood of a child in a larger class being in a larger group of 7–10 children. Results from the qualitative studies extended this picture, by showing the effects this had on teaching and learning, from the teacher's point of view. The answers we got from teachers could be divided into three main categories. They were clear that as groups became bigger, three factors were affected:

- amount and quality of teacher input possible in each group
- the quality of the children's work
- the children's contribution and concentration.

I shall look at each of these in turn.

Amount and quality of teacher input possible in each group

There were many comments about how larger groups adversely affected the nature of teachers' input into groups. Here is a selection of quotes from teachers:

> If I teach larger groups and therefore get around more often, the quality is more likely to be reduced as there are more children working together – all of differing abilities.
>
> (Year 1 teacher)

> In my class we generally work in groups of 7 which is too large. It takes much longer for me to give my attention to each child in the group.
>
> (Reception teacher)

> I feel that the quality of teaching and learning in my class this year is high, due to having a fairly small class of 25 children. This means that for group work, I can [have] small groups which in turn means more individual attention. It has also enabled me to have small groups for the lower ability children, who I feel benefit more from this.
>
> (Reception teacher)

> Having 18–23 children in our class enables us to organize the children in a number of small groups . . . I feel that the children also get more opportunities to experience a 'hands on' approach to their learning and are questioned by the teacher more thoroughly because we are teaching children in smaller groups.
>
> (Year 1 teacher)

Some teachers also felt that the depth of their knowledge about individual children was adversely affected by having larger groups in the class:

> I think getting to know the children is much easier in smaller groups and is fundamental to the smooth running and learning of the children – this must be much better in a smaller class.
>
> (Reception teacher)

Classroom management and control were also affected, according to some teachers, by having larger groups.

> Some of my groups have 10 children – and I often have them working around a large table. It's much harder to control this size group which must affect learning.
>
> (Reception teacher)

The quality of the children's work

The second main category of responses from teachers about the effects of size of group concerned the quality of children's work:

> The quality of what we [do] in group work [is affected] by trying to cater for 7 or 8 in groups to make the class manageable.
>
> (Reception teacher)

There was a view that smaller groups were more effective for certain curriculum areas, such as literacy hour/activities and practical work:

> The children can be taught in small groups and year groups – particularly effective in the literacy hour and practical sessions.
>
> (Year 1 teacher)

> Guided reading is difficult with a group of 6–7 children.
>
> (Reception teacher)

The case studies revealed difficulties faced by teachers:

> The arrangements are fine for literacy hour but when you do maths you think 'now shall I just get them to work as individuals at their own seats or are we going to do musical chairs thing?' It's like a dilemma each time.
>
> (Year 1/2 teacher)

Large group sizes can, therefore, affect the quality of work engaged in by pupils and this can be magnified in certain curriculum areas and task activities, and pose difficult choices for teachers.

The children's contribution and concentration

Larger groups adversely affected the contribution and concentration of children:

> With a group of 6 children, generally, concentration is better and children have more opportunity to contribute . . . in a group of 8 or more those children who are inclined to lose concentration may lapse for longer periods, and have fewer opportunities to contribute.
>
> (Reception teacher)

> My daily routine is not affected by the number of children in my class but the size of groups I work with at any one time is. The bigger the group the easier for individual children to lose concentration, and miss the teaching point.
>
> (Year 1 teacher)

This last quote is interesting in showing that it is group size, rather than the number of children in the class, which affects the teacher's daily routine and the pupils' concentration and ability to grasp points.

The quantitative results suggested that the effects of size of class and group size were most marked in the case of Reception-aged children. Worryingly, teachers' comments indicated that they felt the problems of larger groups were particularly acute for some younger children of Reception age – some (as we have said already) only just 4 years of age.

> Larger groups – young children feel intimidated.
>
> (Reception teacher)

> The quieter children lack confidence and often stay on the fringes during group discussions and activities.
>
> (Reception teacher)

More generally, some teachers felt that with larger groups it was hard to ensure children were progressing well:

> With 5 groups of 6–7 children it is hard to ensure that they are working to their full potential.
>
> (Year 1 teacher)

> I have 30 children which breaks down into 5 groups of 6. This is about manageable. However, if several of the children are absent from the class and groups sizes are brought down to 4 or 5, it makes a tremendous difference.
>
> (Year 1 teacher)

To sum up this section, the interview and questionnaire data indicate a number of educational consequences resulting from the tendency for larger classes to result in larger groups. First, larger groups affected the quantity and quality of teaching in terms of the attention teachers could give each child and group, the quality and effectiveness of their teaching, the thoroughness of their questioning, the amount of extended adult intensive tasks, the depth of their knowledge about individual children, and difficulties with classroom management and control. Second, large group sizes affected the quality of pupils' work. And third, larger groups adversely affected the contribution and concentration of children in groups, particularly in the case of the youngest children in school.

Connections between class size and within-class groupings: what have we learned?

In this chapter I have looked at one way that class and within-class contexts can be linked, by examining connections between class size and the size and number of within-class groupings. It looks as if the youngest children in school have the fewest number of groups, which might have been predicted, but in the largest groups, which seems surprising. It seems likely that at Reception and Year 2, where more adult support is available, pupils may be perceived to be more reliant on adults for the maintenance of concentration and thus the teacher organizes the class into a few large groups so that the ratio of adults to groups is low.

The predominant group size is 4–6 children, which indicates the ubiquity in these English primary schools of classroom organization in terms of small groups. These were followed in frequency by larger groups of 7–10 and 11+ (which were mainly whole classes). The qualitative analyses indicated that smaller groups of 4–6 are favoured by teachers, because of the way it can help teaching input, child concentration and contribution.

A main result from this part of the study is that in larger classes, especially with youngest Reception-aged children, teachers seem forced to teach them in larger groups of 7–10, larger than, according to their own preferences, they would like. The qualitative analyses indicated that larger groups were a less effective educational environment: it was difficult to give children the attention they might want and need from the teacher, and quality of teaching could suffer; the quality of children's work was lower; and their contribution and concentration in groups could suffer, perhaps especially in the case of the youngest children. It seems fair to be concerned that one consequence of larger classes is therefore the likelihood of larger, less educationally effective groups. Lou et al. (1996) also found, on the basis of their meta-analysis of within-class grouping studies, that smaller group sizes were optimal for students' learning; larger groups of 6 to 10 members were less effective.

It might be argued that one solution to teachers' difficulties with large classes would be to alter their approach so that there is more teaching to larger groups or the whole class. This may be possible in some curriculum areas, and for some activities, but, as was argued at the beginning of this chapter, whole class teaching will not always be relevant to primary-aged children, especially the youngest children, who may be more easily distracted.The suggestion that there is more likelihood of whole class teaching in smaller classes should not be taken as support for whole class teaching. Whole class teaching can be used in a productive way, but whole class teaching forced on teachers as a compromise in the face of larger class sizes is a different matter.

It is recognized that there are what researchers will know as validity (or, in more everyday language, accuracy) issues connected to the qualitative component, in that it relies heavily on teachers' perspectives and reported experiences. We were not able to test the relationship between grouping practices and learning in groups in other more objective ways, so the connections identified here have to be treated with caution; nevertheless, the consistency of results stemming from quantitative and qualitative components supports the plausibility of the argument developed in this chapter.

One result that emerged, when looking at the connections between class size and type of interaction within groups, was the finding that there was less cooperative group work in the smallest classes. This ran contrary to our expectation that there would be more evidence of group work in smaller classes. I think that this is a provocative finding. It seems that if smaller classes do have benefits in terms of allowing smaller groups, this is seen almost exclusively by teachers in terms of more focused and individualized teaching in the groups and improved pupil concentration, rather than in terms of any benefits to ways in which children can work together more productively. This is a theme that I shall return to at the end of the book when discussing ways in which teachers can make the most of the opportunities afforded by smaller classes. I return in Chapter 6 to the extent of peer interaction in classes of different sizes.

As said earlier, conceptualization of class size effects has not to date been very sophisticated. The results presented in this chapter indicate a linkage between class size and groupings in the class. So while debate about size of class has often been in terms of reduced size of class resulting in pupil academic gains, it is also important, educationally, to consider *grouping* size, and to ask about the optimum group size, and its effects. This was nicely expressed by the teacher (quoted above) who said that her daily routine was not affected by the number of children in the class but by the size of groups she worked with at any one time.

I return to the role of within-class groupings in connections between class size and children's educational attainments in Chapters 8 and 9.

4 Class size and teaching

In Chapter 1, I described a gap between professional experience and research evidence, when it comes to claims about the connection between class sizes and pupils' educational progress. This gap is perhaps most marked when it comes to effects of class size on teaching. Many teachers feel that teaching and learning are likely to be improved in smaller classes, but (as we saw in Chapter 2) the evidence from research is not clear-cut; some even suggests that although teachers may feel their teaching has benefited in small classes, this is not supported by observational data. A main motivation for the research reported in this chapter was to gain insights that might help inform this gap.

In this chapter I am interested in just one aspect of teaching – the moment-by-moment interactions during the school day between teachers and their pupils. Arends (1994) lists three main aspects of teaching: executive interactive and organizational functions. Our concern here is with the interactive functions of teaching.

Our work in this area has been informed by three general approaches to teaching:

- teaching time allocation
- research on effective teaching
- cognitive approaches to teaching.

Teaching time allocation

Research on teaching has a long and varied history, and studies are far too numerous to be reviewed here. A central position of much research and comment is the importance of maximizing teaching time and instructional support for children's learning (Brophy and Good 1986; Creemers 1994; Pellegrini and Blatchford 2000). On logical and common-sense grounds it seems likely that the number of children in a class will increase the amount of time that teachers spend in procedural and domestic matters such as taking the register, lining children up and putting on coats, dealing with domestic duties such as toileting, accidents and so on, and conversely decrease the amount of time that can be spent on instruction and dealing with individual children. It might be expected to be particularly important to maximize the amount of teaching and individual support for the youngest children in school.

This expectation is consistent with teachers' views. In the UK a survey of teachers' and head teachers' views showed that practitioners believe that large class sizes affect teaching and learning, and they were particularly aware that larger classes could have an adverse effect on the amount of teacher attention (Bennett 1996). In the USA, it was concluded on the basis of teacher interviews conducted in the STAR research project that:

> A common benefit cited by teachers in small and regular plus aide classes was that they were better able to individualize instruction. These teachers reported increased monitoring of student behavior and learning, opportunities for more immediate and more individualized re-teaching, more enrichment, more frequent interactions with each child, a better match between each child's ability and the instructional opportunities provided, a more detailed knowledge of each child's needs as a learner, and more time to meet individual learners' needs using a variety of instructional approaches.
>
> (Pate-Bain et al. 1992: 254)

Teachers' reports are supported by an analysis conducted by Glass et al. (1982) which found that smaller classes resulted in greater teacher knowledge of pupils, frequency of one-to-one contacts between teachers and pupils, variety of activities, adaptation of teaching to individual pupils, and opportunities to talk to parents (Cooper 1989). Other studies report more individual teaching and attention (Harder 1990; Turner 1990; Pate-Bain et al. 1992), and more feedback (Cooper 1989; Pate-Bain et al. 1992). However, in direct contrast to teacher views, a widely cited study found no statistically significant differences between class sizes for most teacher activities (Shapson et al. 1980).

There have been several more recent US studies that have examined the effects of class size on teaching. Molnar and colleagues (1999) report results from the Wisconsin Student Achievement Guarantee in Education (SAGE) project – a follow-up study of children from kindergarten to grade 3, begun in the 1996/97 school year. Though not a study of class size reduction as such, the programme required participating schools to implement four interventions, one of which involved pupil–teacher ratio reductions to 15 students per teacher. Teachers were asked to rank items in terms of the extent to which they were affected by reduced class size. The teacher behaviours that received the highest rankings were more individualized instruction; more teaching time; more discussion, sharing and answering; more hands-on activities and more content coverage. Interviews conducted with 28 SAGE teachers suggested that small classes allowed more knowledge of students, reduced problems with classroom discipline, allowed more time on instruction, and more individualization, for example, involving more one-to-one help. The most important classroom process affected by reduced class size, therefore, seems to be individualization. From this, Molnar et al. (1999) put forward a tentative model of teaching in small classes which includes three elements: better knowledge of students, more instructional time, and teacher satisfaction, and these in turn lead to more individualized instruction.

In a small-scale study of two matched schools, one with small classes (about 14 students) and one with larger classes (about 24 students) Achilles and his colleagues report on differences in teacher behaviour. On the basis of a systematic observation study of mainly grade 1 classes, they report increases over the school year in teacher time on task in the small class, but decreases over the year in teacher time on task in the larger classes (see Achilles 1999).

In another study, Betts and Shkolnik (1999) analysed relationships between class size and teacher time allocation, based on a secondary analysis of a national survey of students in middle and high schools in the USA (the survey covered the period 1987 to 1992, so is rather dated now). Data came from a survey of mathematics teachers who completed forms describing their classes the previous autumn. Teachers were asked to retrospectively estimate minutes per week in group instruction (it is not clear if this includes whole class teaching), individual instruction per student, and percentage time in instructional activities. Results show some evidence that teachers substitute group instruction for individual instruction as class size increases, and devote less time to group instruction and more on individual instruction in smaller classes. There was a small effect on percentage overall instructional time. They argue that teachers would make better use of small classes if they did not reduce group instruction, though they agree that further research is needed to identify exactly what changes in teaching style might be most effective.

Rice (1999) also conducted a secondary analysis of teacher survey data on students transferring to high school. The study is based on high school mathematics and science teachers' estimates of percentage time devoted to several activities, including instructing small groups and individuals, time devoted to innovative instruction and time devoted to whole group discussion. Findings showed that in mathematics as class size increased, less time was spent on small groups and individuals, innovative instructional practices and whole group discussions, though increases in class sizes beyond 20 had little effect. There were no relationships between class size and instructional time allocation measures in science.

Both these studies raise interesting questions about the effect of class size differences on teaching and non-teaching (for example procedural/managerial) time overall, and also on how it is shared between individuals, groups and the whole class. But the studies are limited in that they rely on a secondary analysis of rather general teacher retrospective estimates of time spent. Basic distinctions, for example, between individual, group and class contexts, which might be expected to be differently affected by class size, are not always clear. Another problem with the studies is the age of students involved. We have seen that the strongest effects are reported with younger children and especially children immediately after entry to school, and so results involving much older children may underestimate effects of class size differences and/or involve different processes.

Research on effective teaching

There is of course more to research on teaching than time allocation. There has been a lot of research, going back decades, seeking to identify aspects of effective teaching, and more recently allied to research on effective schooling (as reviewed by Brophy and Good 1986; Creemers 1994; Galton et al. 1999, and many others). But, again, there has been relatively little interest in classroom contextual influences such as class size. For the most part the underlying model is a direct one with a focus on the effects of teaching on pupil achievement. In Dunkin and Biddle's (1974) model, which has been influential in research on teaching, there were four stages – 'presage', 'context', 'process' and 'product'. Class size, in this model, is one of several 'context' variables. This model helps to position class size in the context of overall influences on children's progress, but there has been little research that has actually studied connections between class size and the 'processes' within classrooms, which will include teacher and pupil behaviour.

There is very little UK research on the effects of class size differences on teaching. In an intriguing but small-scale study, lessons taught by four teachers from the maintained sector were compared when teaching their own class, half their class and a smaller class in a private school, and were then contrasted with five teachers from the independent sector teaching their own small class and a larger class in the maintained sector (Galton et al. 1996). The authors claim that in smaller classes there are more sustained interactions between teacher and child, more time on task than routine management, and more feedback on work. The results are difficult to interpret because they involve only a handful of teachers under unusual circumstances and for brief periods; moreover, none of the results reported appear to have reached statistical significance.

Cognitive approaches to teaching

A quite different approach to teaching, with roots more in cognitive psychology, has drawn on the ideas of the Russian psychologist Lev Vygotsky, and has highlighted the importance of what has been called 'scaffolding' to inform effective teaching and tutoring (see Tharp and Gallimore 1991; Meadows 1996; Wood and Wood 1996; Wood 1998). This line of thought suggests that effective learning takes place when contingency, feedback and assisted learning are provided and a number of authors show that this is best done not in school contexts, but rather in more informal contacts in the home. The underlying learning context in this tradition of thought is the one-to-one tutoring relationship. From this point of view the school classroom seems inherently disadvantaged as a site able to provide a rich learning environment, and a classroom with a large number of young children is particularly problematic. However, connections with numbers of children in the class have not been worked through conceptually or empirically.

Drawing on previous research and theory two general questions informed the research described in this chapter:

- Do teachers in large and small classes differ in terms of time spent in teaching/instructional activities overall, time in individual, group and class contexts; and the amount of teacher–child contact and individual attention from teachers?
- Apart from these more obviously quantitative dimensions, do teachers in large and small classes differ in terms of more qualitative dimensions of teaching, seen in interactions between teachers and children?

As described in Chapter 2, it seemed to us that an advance in understanding connections between class size and teaching would be to use a multi-method approach, in particular to integrate teachers' judgements and experiences with case studies, and also make use of carefully designed time allocation estimates as well as systematic observation data. As a general strategy it seemed to us important to consider different approaches not in opposition to each other but as complementary.

Results

In this part of the study we made use of four of the types of data described in Chapter 2, that is – end of year questionnaires, case studies, termly 'time allocation' variables and systematic observations. Each of these types of data were analysed and separate reports compiled. I shall summarize results from each in turn, with the aim of identifying and integrating the most common and consistent themes across different forms of data collection.

I begin with results from the teachers' end of year questionnaires.

Teachers' experiences of the effect of class size on teaching and learning: data from end of year questionnaires

The end of year questionnaire responses to the question concerning ways in which teachers said teaching and learning were affected by the number of children in their class were analysed as described in Chapter 2. The frequencies for each of the 19 categories that were identified were calculated as well as the percentage of teachers who gave this category. A full breakdown of these results is not provided here, but the most frequent three responses given by more than 10 per cent of teachers during any year were:

- less individual attention/contact/feedback
- less group attention/larger group sizes
- fewer individual reading opportunities.

The single most prevalent of the 19 categories was that in larger classes teachers were able to give less attention and feedback to individual children in the class. This category is of particular relevance to this chapter and in this section I describe the most prevalent types of teachers' responses that were classified. Each type is described and illustrated with quotes, representative of many similar quotes drawn from the reports. They detail a compelling account of ways teachers felt that attention to pupils was affected by the number of children in their classes.

Amount, duration and extended nature of interactions

Teachers were concerned that more children in the class affected the quantity of educational interaction each child received. That is, the more children in the class, the less individual teaching was seen to be possible. This was seen as an almost mathematically necessary consequence:

> More children = less time for each child. Simple division really!

and

> Bigger class = smaller proportion of my time!

One teacher of a large class used a different kind of image: she described her professional self as

> like Marmite, spread very thinly.

Another teacher said that in her large class there was

> less opportunity for one-to-one teaching, which is essential,

while conversely, a teacher of a smaller class was clear that

> a smaller class has enabled me to spend longer with each child.

Quality and intensity of interactions

Not only does the quantity of interaction decrease when classes are large, but also teachers feel that the quality of these interactions is affected:

> Children have less quality time with the teacher.

A Reception class teacher in a small class made the following comment:

> The greatest difference, however, is in the time and quality of support that can be given to each child.

Teachers often made comments concerning their affective response to class sizes and this highlighted the emotional work of teachers and the feelings they have towards children in their classes.

Monitoring, checking children's understandings and offering appropriate feedback to individuals

Allied to comments from teachers working in large classes concerning the decline in quality of interactions with children, were the types of interactions that they felt to be valuable. Teachers wrote that monitoring, checking understanding, and offering appropriate feedback to individual children was more difficult in a larger class, implying that these were considered to be important aspects of teaching that, if neglected, have a detrimental effect on learning. Teachers valued being able to offer immediate feedback on children's work, and felt this was more difficult with large classes:

> Marking work alongside the child is not always possible

and

> With a smaller class pupils get faster feedback on their achievements.

Supporting individual learning

Comments from teachers of both large and small classes suggested that they perceived a relationship between the number of children in their classes and the support for learning that could be achieved. A Reception class teacher with a smaller class wrote:

> I feel that I have been able to work through problems as and when they arise, far more successfully. This has given the children a secure and settled start to school, allowing them to become independent and confident in their abilities.

This theme was continued by a Year 1 teacher with a small class, who valued the fact that she could spend more time with individual children and encourage children

> to work independently and at their own level.

Other teachers with small classes wrote about getting to know the children very well and being able to support their particular learning needs.

Perhaps the single theme that underlies these comments from teachers is that with fewer children in the class there is more time possible with children to support their educational progress.

Extent and depth of knowledge of individual children

Teachers of larger classes were concerned that they could not develop a depth of knowledge and understanding of the children as individuals. Once again, this category reflects the view of primary school teachers that their work is not only about more than enabling children to achieve educationally, but also encompasses social and emotional areas of development. We can contrast a quote from a teacher with a large class:

> There is less time for individuals, to listen to their news, to get to know them,

with that from a teacher with a smaller class:

> Demands on time being lessened has meant better relationships with all the children – I feel I know more about their individual likes and dislikes, and personalities.

Case studies

On the basis of the fieldworkers' reports, organized under the main headings for observations, interviews with teachers and head teachers (as described in

Chapter 2), a composite report was written which identified main themes. In this section I summarize just that part of the report concerned with teacher–pupil interactions and knowledge of children. The following sub-themes were identified as central in summarizing field-notes and conclusions by fieldworkers:

- amount of individual attention
- immediacy and responsiveness of teacher response to children
- sustained and purposeful interactions
- dealing with interruptions
- depth of knowledge of children
- disruption and noise
- sensitivity to individuals' particular needs
- teaching in whole class situations
- flexibility of teacher questioning techniques.

It can be seen immediately that there are overlaps with these themes and the teachers' comments from the questionnaires. This was despite the questionnaires being analysed by different researchers. There is not sufficient space to go through each of these categories in turn. By way of illustration, and to complement the material in the last section, I concentrate on three case studies but draw on others where appropriate. The themes that emerge are to a degree typical, and occurred regularly in the case studies, but the purpose of the case studies and this section is to bring out the particular experiences of teachers and children in individual classrooms. The first is a teacher in a large class and the two others are teachers in small classes.

Large class (Year 1)

This was a one-form-entry village school in a largely rural LEA with a predominantly middle-class and white intake. There were 37 children on roll in Year 1, although at the time the observations were conducted, this number had been reduced to 35. The teacher had taught for 13 years, 8 of these at the current school, and was due to leave at the end of the term to take up a deputy headship. The teacher had taught the class in their Reception year and knew them very well. The case study gives some insight into the difficulties that teachers in large classes might face.

Despite this teacher's experience and competence, she was stressed and admitted to being 'worn out'. She spent many hours outside her contact time marking and she read with children individually in her lunch break. The observation notes indicated that effective teaching was evident in this large class but at great personal and emotional expense in terms of an eroding of the teacher's personal time. The observer noted that this particular teacher had interactions with about 17 children every minute, which was exhausting for her. The observer noted that classroom interaction tended to consist of the teacher telling the children things rather than sustained or meaningful interaction about tasks or concepts. In one extract, involving writing activities, the observer's notes show the teacher attending to lots of different children for short lengths of time, often repeating instructions. The teacher–child interactions were also concerned with 'management' activities, and quelling rising noise levels. As noise levels rose easily to unacceptable levels, when everyone was talking, she had to keep them all quieter than she wanted. There was a similar problem, seen in one instance, when children assembled on the carpet to talk about their work, and the teacher was irritated by the noise of all their papers rustling. This, along with other examples, did not seem to be an effective use of her considerable skills and time, and she admitted to becoming frustrated and tired. She was forced to talk almost all the time.

Additionally, the researcher noted that the behaviour of the children could be strained. This was related to the limited amount of space that the young children had to move in. Children in the classroom were often grouped by ability, but the groups were, inevitably, large and included a wide range of ability. This made differentiation of tasks difficult and there was evidence that the higher ability children were not making the progress expected of them.

Other case studies of large classes showed similar difficulties, and showed individual feedback was limited. In one class of 32 children, the teacher was observed to interact well with the children, listening to their questions and encouraging them to join in with discussions, but with so many in the class it was difficult to involve many of them in, for example, practical examples when doing number work. The teacher felt that with so many children she was not able to talk to each child every day, and that children received less individual attention than they would in a smaller class.

Small classes

By contrast, in one very small class of 15 children a particular feature noted by the observer was the amount of interaction between the teacher and the children and the responsiveness of the teacher to the children's interests, which she fed effectively into her teaching. Significantly, the children asked many questions which the teacher was able to respond to and make part of the teaching session. The teacher believed that this was partly due to the size of the group, as she could listen to them all and respond to them. This increased their confidence and enabled them to feel secure enough to ask questions. During a history lesson observed by the researcher, the children were asked to recall their visit to a Victorian classroom. One child asked what the children did when it became dark, especially in the winter, as they had no electricity. The teacher made a teaching point of this and a discussion ensued. More children asked questions and others offered possible solutions, such as the use of candles. The activity that the teacher had planned was open ended enough for this new aspect to be reflected by the children in their recording. This suggests that in smaller classes teaching can be more flexible.

The teacher was also able to give immediate feedback to the children about the quality of their work. Because the class was so small, the children rarely had to wait for support or feedback and this ensured that they were consistently on task and not distracted. The children also showed high levels of persistence, which owed much to the teacher being able to give them the appropriate help at the right time. The teacher demonstrated considerable sensitivity and was able to ascertain which children needed help very quickly.

Observations in another small class of fewer than 15 children showed that interactions between the teacher and the children were of high quality in both whole class and small group contexts. There was an efficient atmosphere that was at the same time warm and encouraging. The children were taken through the work to be done in a detailed and clear way. There was a lot of attention given to many of the children. Perhaps the central feature was the sustained nature of interactions in whole class sessions, and their purposeful nature. There is no real test of this but it was the observer's view that the small class allowed this to happen without strain on the teacher. The sustained nature of teacher–pupil contact was also evident in small group contexts. A distinctive feature was the way the teacher stayed with the group sometimes for the whole session, even when they had started independent work, still encouraging and prompting, and answering their questions, and seeing the work through to its completion.

The sustained nature of teacher–child interactions in whole class teaching sessions, with a carry over into subsequent individual and group work, was also a feature of another smaller class of just over 20 children. When introducing a writing activity during the literacy hour on the third observation day, the teacher modelled the process and the children were asked questions about what she was writing. When the groups were sent off to work, the teacher checked their understanding of the tasks to be completed. She also often checked with individual children (especially with those in the support group) to ensure they had understood the concepts being presented and had understood the task to be completed. If required, these interactions were of a reasonable duration (up to four or five minutes). The teacher recognized that some individuals did claim more of her time than others, but this was related to their academic needs and not behavioural ones.

A connected theme was more effective and flexible use of questioning techniques found in whole class sessions in small classes. In one class of 17 children, the whole class sessions observed during the three observation days were in excess of 25 minutes long. The children's attention was maintained throughout by the teacher, who encouraged contributions from all of them. On the third observation day the teacher used two big books written by Judith Kerr to compare the stories. The teacher asked open questions, accepting all answers and reframing them as necessary; for example, one child talked about the wild animals that were in the story, and, through questioning, the child was able to realize that these were part of a dream that one of the characters was having. The teacher emphasized phrasing and sentence structure, not by correcting but by modelling and rephrasing the answers the children gave. When the teacher wanted to teach or revise particular vocabulary, she asked more specific and closed questions, for example when she wanted to teach different fiction genres, such as adventure stories and traditional tales. This situation contrasts markedly with the situation in large classes where questioning more often seemed to have a controlling purpose.

But observations in another small class of 20 children also showed one possible drawback, stemming from the potential in smaller classes for more immediate feedback, which was identified in several of the case studies, and which makes the important point that size of class does not *necessarily* lead to positive effects. It was noticeable in this class, even during whole class carpet sessions, that the teacher made time for individual interactions and was able to correct small things such as pronunciation. The teacher was able to give effective feedback to almost all children all the time and they came to her even while she was working with a group. However, this tendency to respond immediately to children indicates one potential cost of smaller classes, in that it took up lesson time and interrupted the flow of activities. The observer also noted that adults such as the secretary, helpers and nurse were allowed to interrupt the teaching in a way that was clearly not beneficial to the children.

Termly questionnaires: time estimates

I now turn to the two more obviously quantitative forms of data collection. Analysis of data from the termly questionnaire showed that there was a moderate but significant relationship between class size and the percentage of time spent teaching overall (that is, teaching whole classes, groups and individual teaching added together), at Reception and Y1. The association was in the same direction for Y2 but not significant (see Blatchford et al. 2002c). These results mean that there was a consistent, albeit not strong, tendency over the first three years of schooling for children in smaller classes to experience more teaching time overall. Because of the way the variables were defined, these results also mean that there was a (positive) correlation of the same order between size of class and non-teaching time. That is, the larger the class the more time spent in non-teaching activities, like taking the register and so forth.

The association between class size and teaching time can be looked at in a more precise way by showing the connection graphically. This is done in Figure 4.1 for the Reception year. Here the percentage teaching time associated with a particular class size can be easily read from the graph. If we compare

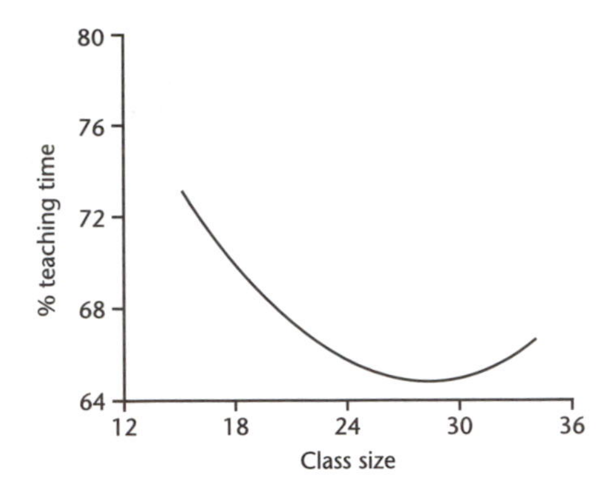

Figure 4.1 Relationship between class size and percentage teaching time in Reception

class sizes of 20 with 30 we find that in the smaller class size teachers spend nearly 70 per cent of their time on teaching while in the larger class they spend just under 65 per cent. In classes over 30 there is slight tendency for the amount of teaching time to increase, though there are not many classes at the extremes of the class size distributions and not too much should be read into this trend. The overall relationship is that teaching time tends to increase as class size decreases. Associations between class size and teaching time for Year 1 are similar and are not shown.

Separate analyses of associations between class size and percentage time teaching individuals, groups and whole classes did not show a consistent picture.

To sum up this section: there was consistent, albeit not strong, evidence from the termly questionnaire that class size was related to the amount of teaching overall.

Systematic observations

First I look at the three 'social modes', that is, teacher–child interactions, child–child interactions and behaviour when not interacting. Total scores for these three categories were calculated for each child by adding together all the sub-categories within each. Figure 4.2 shows differences between large and small classes in the average number of observations per child for these three categories.

It can be seen in Figure 4.2 that children in small classes were more often observed interacting with their teachers than were children in large classes. In a small class children were observed on average 213 times with their teacher, as compared to 144 times in a large class. I look at the other two modes – child–child interactions and not interacting – in Chapter 5.

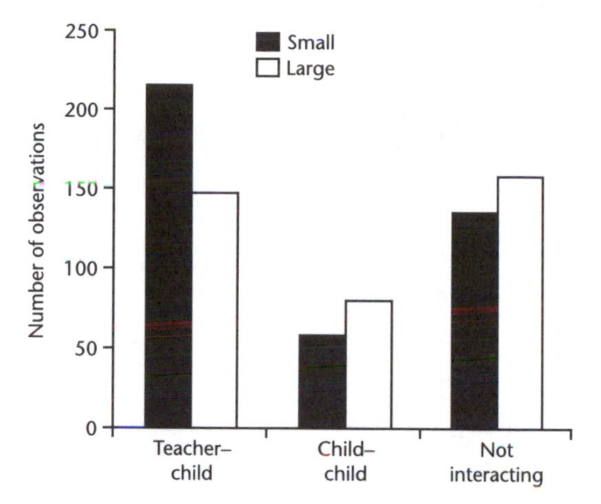

Figure 4.2 Frequency of observations in the three 'social modes' – teacher–child, child–child and not interacting: differences between large and small classes

Looking more closely at the teacher to child categories, it can be seen in Figure 4.3 that children in smaller classes were more likely to interact with their teachers on a one-to-one basis (on average 36 versus 18 observations) and in groups (77 versus 35 observations). There were no differences between large and small classes in the amount of whole class teaching.

The child was more likely to be the 'focus' of a teacher's attention in a

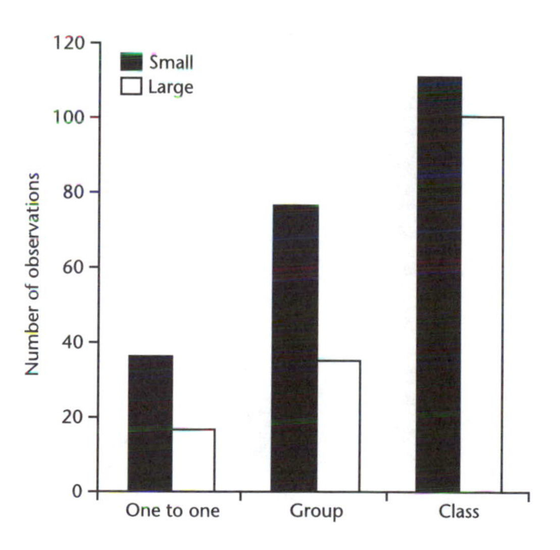

Figure 4.3 Frequency of observations in social setting of teacher-to-child interactions: differences between large and small classes

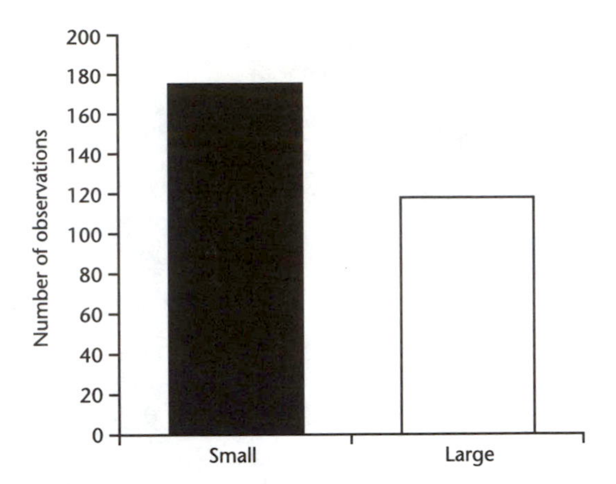

Figure 4.4 Frequency of observations in teacher-to-child interactions – child is focus of teacher's attention: differences between large and small classes

small compared to large class (on average 173 versus 117 observations – see Figure 4.4); that is to say, the child was the subject of a teacher's attention on a one-to-one basis (by definition the child was the focus), or in a group or the whole class.

Children in small classes also experienced more teaching overall (see Figure 4.5). Just taking the category 'task teach', which might be considered

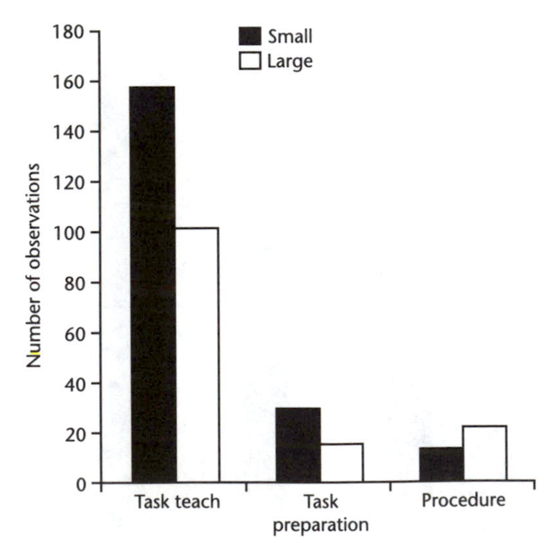

Figure 4.5 Frequency of observations in types of teacher-to-child interactions: differences between large and small classes

the most strict definition of teaching, in the sense that it denotes contacts directly concerned with the substantive content of children's task activities (communicating concepts, facts or ideas by explaining, informing, demonstrating, questioning, and so on), rather than setting them up (task preparation) or getting materials ready (procedure), we see that this was coded on average 156 times per child in small classes but 101 times in large classes. There was also about twice as much teacher 'task preparation' in small as opposed to large classes. The only category of teacher talk to children that was more numerous in larger classes was procedural talk, as predicted.

The categories used to describe children's contacts directed at their teachers are given in Figures 4.6 to 4.8. There was more attending to the teacher (144 versus 96 – see Figure 4.7), responding (27 versus 22) and more initiating (8 versus 6 although this category was not common – see Figure 4.6) in small classes. So children had a more active role in interaction with their teachers (respond plus initiate), and were more attentive to them (attend).

Figure 4.8 also shows results covering the content of the behaviour. As with the teacher to child categories, there is more task-related talk (166 versus 107) and more social talk to teachers in small classes. There was also more inappropriate and off-task behaviour (usually not attending to the teacher) in larger classes.

To sum up the systematic observation results on teacher–child interaction: in small classes there was more one-to-one teaching, more teaching in

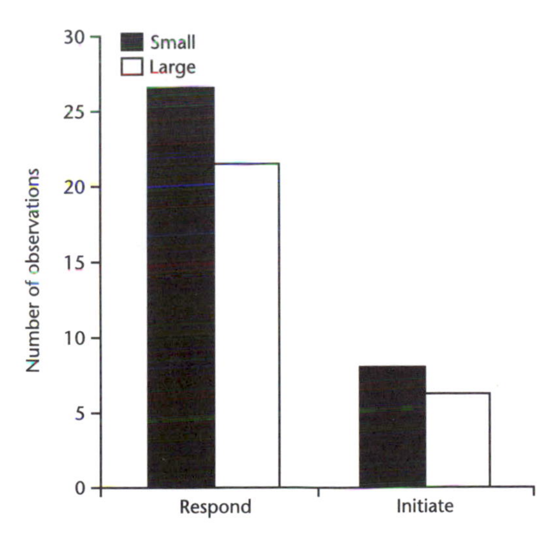

Figure 4.6 Frequency of observations in child-to-teacher responses and initiations: differences between large and small classes

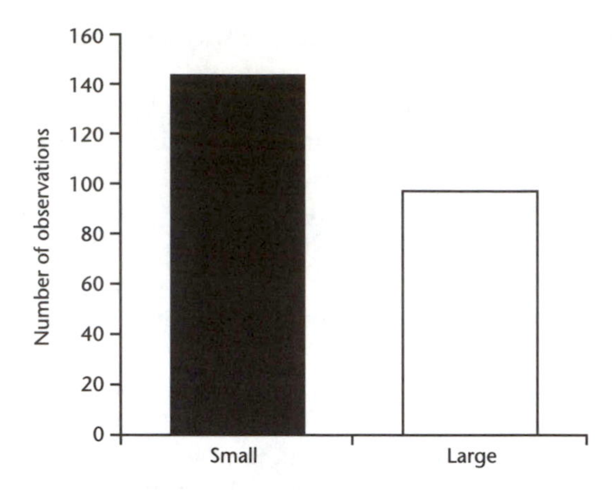

Figure 4.7 Frequency of observations in child attends to teacher: differences between large and small classes

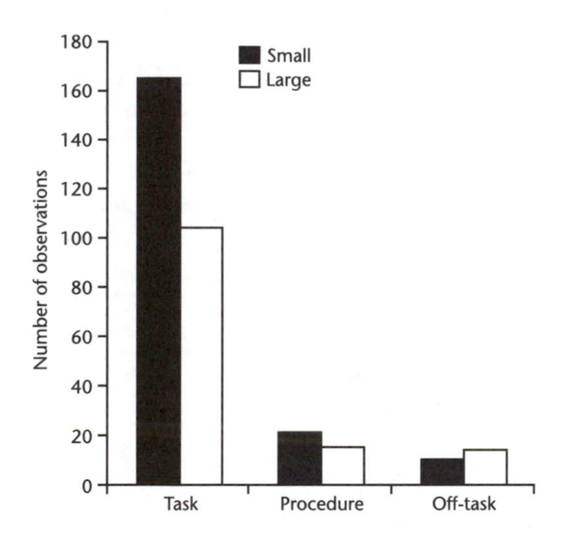

Figure 4.8 Frequency of observations in types of child-to-teacher interactions: differences between large and small classes

groups (but not more or less teaching in whole class contexts), more times when they were the focus of a teacher's attention (whatever the context), more time interacting with their teachers and more teaching overall, and more time actively involved in interactions with their teachers (that is, responding or initiating rather than just attending).

Class size and teaching: conclusions

The results from the two more obviously quantitative components, especially the systematic observations, seemed clear. There was consistent evidence that children in small classes were more likely to interact with their teachers, there was more teaching on a one-to-one basis, more times when children were the focus of a teacher's attention, more teaching overall, and more times when children were attending to the teacher and actively involved in interactions with them (that is, responding or initiating rather than just attending). These results therefore show that individual children in small classes receive more interactions with their teachers of a task-related nature.

These results seem to support an interpretation of class size effects in terms of teacher time allocation. The termly questionnaires and the systematic observations show that more time is spent in teaching in smaller classes. This suggests a kind of 'dilution' theory as seen, for example, in research on family size. Meadows (1996) explains family size effects on children's development in terms of the parents' effect being diluted if they spread themselves between many children.

Although not shown in the results presented in this chapter, children also receive more interactions from their teachers of a social or personal nature in small classes, indicating that the interactions are more personalized. The fact that there are fewer teacher interactions about procedural matters adds to this picture. Overall in smaller classes children seem to experience interactions that are both more work (particularly) and socially intense. Turning this on its head, in a large class an individual child will, by comparison, experience a less intense contact with their teacher, receiving fewer work and social contacts but more contacts about procedural matters.

The results indicate that children in small classes have a more active involvement in interactions with their teachers, as indexed by the greater number of initiations and responses. The trend toward individualization in small classes is not therefore indicative of a passive role for children; the opposite seems more likely, that is to say, children in large classes spend less time actively interacting.

I have also looked in this chapter at teaching interactions in a more rounded way, allowed by the end of year questionnaire and case study analyses. Results from the end of year questionnaires and case studies complemented this picture by providing a broader and more qualitative version of connections between class size and teaching. These components suggested that class size affected the amount of individual attention, the immediacy and responsiveness of teachers to children, the sustained and purposeful nature of interaction between teachers and children, the depth of a teacher's knowledge of children in her class, and sensitivity to individual children's particular needs.

Overall, taking data from all four sources, we propose that there is support for the notion that in smaller classes there is more likelihood of what we can call *teacher support for learning*. One aspect of this is more likelihood of individualized teaching in small classes. In general these results appear consistent with other studies reviewed earlier. We need, though, to be clear about the nature of individualization affected by small classes compared to large. Although there is more one-to-one teaching in small classes, the greater incidence of times when the child was the 'focus' of attention indicates that children receive more attention in group and whole class situations as well. This needs to be borne in mind when considering worries that smaller classes might encourage a reliance on individual teaching.

The effects of class size on teaching can be seen in terms of research on effective teaching. Small classes may encourage aspects of teaching that are the same as those identified in research on effective teaching (for example immediate feedback, sustained purposeful interactions) linked with the promotion of pupil achievement (a point made by Galton et al. 1996). The connection will not necessarily follow, and small classes will not necessarily make a bad teacher better, but small classes seem likely to make it easier for teachers to be effective.

The connection between class size and teaching can also be seen in terms of cognitive approaches to teaching, considered briefly at the beginning of this chapter. Many of the teaching characteristics affected by size of class can be seen as aspects of 'scaffolding', a term associated with Vygotsky, but originally used by Wood and Bruner in the late 1970s when considering mother–child interactions (see Wood 1998). Much of what we found in the case studies and end of year questionnaire reports, for example, regarding individual attention, immediacy of feedback, sustained interactions, flexible and effective questioning techniques, can be seen as instances of scaffolding. Again, the connection cannot be said to be proven, and it will not follow necessarily, but there is a strong suggestion that in a small class teachers will more easily be able to provide effective scaffolding for their pupils. A large class, on the other hand, is likely to make such individually supportive interactions with pupils very difficult, especially if control becomes an issue and dominates interactions. Scaffolding is likely to be most important in the early years of schooling, when it needs to be at its most active and sustained. I shall return to the effects of class size on teaching in Chapter 9.

5 The effect of class size on support for reading

In this chapter I look more specifically at one type of classroom process likely to be affected by class size differences – individual support for reading, in the form of adults in the classroom hearing individual children read. On logical and common-sense grounds it seems likely that the number of children in a class will affect the amount of time that can be spent on instruction and dealing with individual children. It might be expected to be particularly important to maximize individual support for the youngest children in school, during Reception and KS1 (4–7 years), and so effects of class size differences may be most marked at this stage.

As part of an earlier study of the teaching of reading in three LEAs it was found that the two most common reading activities were reading to the whole class and hearing children read individually (Ireson and Blatchford 1993). Nearly one half of teachers in this survey said they heard each child read once a week, one-third between two and four times, and 16 per cent daily. Just over half of the teachers said they heard individual children read from between 5 and 10 minutes, one-fifth for less than 5 minutes and 7 per cent for 11 minutes or more.

These findings indicate that the strategy of hearing individual children read was, until recently anyway, a main part of the teaching of reading. There has been for some time a debate about the success of this strategy, and concern over the most effective and efficient ways of hearing children read. One limitation of short sessions is that they may be relatively superficial, with little opportunity to explore each child's understanding of text (Ireson and Blatchford 1993). Some have argued that efforts should be made to extend the length of each session, in order to provide a more thorough analysis of, and feedback on, each child's reading (Ireson and Blatchford 1993).

Recent strategies concerning literacy, introduced in the UK, appear to have profound consequences for the strategy of hearing children read. The stress is now on a more structured approach involving whole class teaching and structured group reading, and a set of prescribed activities. The role of teachers when it comes to individual support for reading is now more problematic. I return to the changed context for literacy teaching at the end of this chapter.

Whatever the arguments for and against the educational efficacy of individual support for reading, teachers often still see it as a main part of the teaching of reading at Reception and KS1 (Moriarty et al. 2001). It is through careful monitoring on an individual basis of children's first efforts at reading out loud that they can assess children's successes and areas where they need assistance. In this chapter I ask whether class size differences affect the frequency and length of time children are heard to read, as well as more fine-grained dimensions such as teacher feedback. I also ask how connections between class size and individual support for reading, as a part of teaching and learning in the classroom, are perceived by teachers.

Research approach

As we saw in Chapter 2, there were a number of forms of data collected in the study. In this chapter we made use of three types of data: first, teacher estimates of the frequency and duration of reading aloud to an adult in school, second, teacher end of year reports, and third, case studies conducted by fieldworkers.

Results

Each of the three forms of data have been analysed and separate reports compiled. Here I summarize results from each of these forms of data in turn, with the aim of identifying and integrating the most common and consistent themes across different forms of data collection.

Termly questionnaire results

Descriptive data on frequency and durations – in terms of the four levels of frequency and duration of reading aloud to an adult in school, for Reception, Year 1 and Year 2, are shown in Table 5.1

It can be seen that for all three years the most prevalent trend was for children to be heard to read once or twice per week, while in about one-third of Reception and Y1 classes children were heard to read three or four times per week. With regard to the duration of sessions, there was a tendency for children to be heard for 10–20 minutes, and rarely less than 5 minutes.

Associations were then calculated between class size, pupil staff and pupil adult and the two hearing children read variables, that is frequency

Table 5.1 Frequency and duration of hearing children read: Reception, Year 1 and Year 2

Frequency	*Reception*	*Year 1*	*Year 2*
Daily	35	26	6
	13%	13%	5%
3–4 times per week	97	74	15
	35%	37%	13%
1–2 times per week	146	95	78
	52%	47%	67%
Less than weekly	2	8	18
	1%	4%	15%
Total n	280	203	117

Duration	*Reception*	*Year 1*	*Year 2*
Less than 5 minutes	1	4	6
	0%	2%	5%
5–10 minutes	53	45	33
	19%	22%	28%
10–20 minutes	174	106	53
	63%	51%	45%
More than 20 minutes	50	52	26
	18%	25%	22%
Total n	278	207	118

and duration per week. I shall not present these results in full here but they can be summarized as showing a consistent tendency for children in the Reception year and Year 1 to be heard to read more frequently and for more time per week as class sizes became smaller. Conversely, as class sizes increased, the frequency and amount of time hearing children read decreased. There was no sign of significant associations between class size and hearing children read in Year 2, and no sign of any connection between pupil–staff and pupil–adult ratios and hearing children read, for any year.

In order to be more specific about the effects of class size on the frequency of being heard to read, the relationship between class size and the chance of being heard to read three or more times per week (that is, adding together the most frequent categories) in the Reception year is expressed graphically in Figure 5.1. The graph shows an overall tendency for children to be heard to read most frequently in smaller classes. In a class with 20 pupils, there is a 55 per cent chance children will be heard to read frequently (three or more times per week), while in a class with 30 pupils the chance is only 25 per cent.

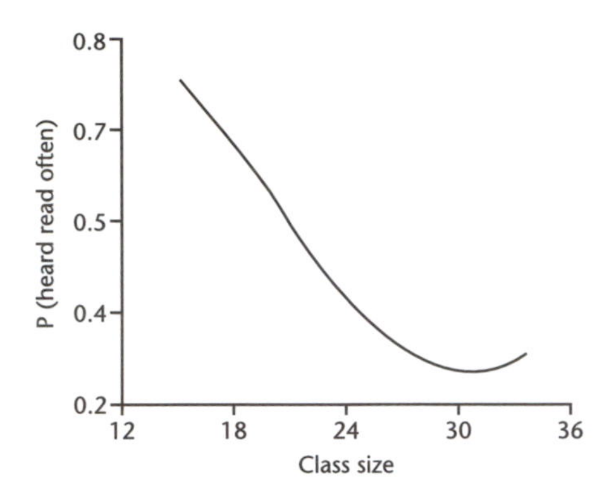

Figure 5.1 Relationship between class size and the probability of being heard read (more than three times per week in the Reception year)

Children in the smaller classes are, therefore, heard to read more frequently. In the case of the length of time heard to read in the Reception year, 43 per cent of teachers in classes of 20 or fewer heard children read for 20 minutes on more per week, while in classes with 31 or more this figure is only 8 per cent. Children in the largest classes were more likely to be heard to read for the briefest periods – 5 minutes or less per week and 5–10 minutes per week (both categories together amounted to 36 per cent as opposed to 12 per cent in classes of 20 or less).

Results for Y1 are similar and to avoid repetition I shall not give details here.

There is, therefore, general support for the view that size of class, at least during the Reception year and Year 1, affects one main aspect of the teaching of reading; as class size decreases, children are heard to read more often, and for longer periods of time each week.

Results from end of year questionnaires

The end of year questionnaire responses to the question concerning ways in which teachers said teaching and learning were affected by the number of children in their class were analysed for main categories and then frequencies and percentages were calculated (as described in Chapters 2 and 4). We saw in Chapter 4 that the most common way that teachers felt that class size influenced the quality of teaching and learning was through the reduced time for educational interactions, and this includes individual reading support. This was by far the most prevalent of the collective categories, taking up more than 50 per cent of all responses at each age level.

In this section we concentrate on responses coded in the category 'fewer individual reading opportunities', and illustrate these with representative quotes from the questionnaires, but also extend this by drawing, where appropriate, from the other two main categories of response (see Chapter 4).

First of all it is worth noting again teachers' general belief that in large classes there is less time to spend with individual children, and this included teacher support for individual children's reading development. Reception teachers in particular were clear about the importance of listening to individual reading on a regular basis, in order to monitor children's reading progress, and plan effective individual reading programmes. In larger classes teachers felt they were less likely to find the time to carry out this particular task.

> It takes me all week to hear my children read once.

> Hearing children read in a big class is obviously very difficult on a very frequent basis because of the demands of all the other curriculum areas.

> [In a small class] working with small numbers has meant children have been given more individual time – for reading/shared reading on a more frequent basis.

The following quote is instructive because it comes from a Reception teacher who saw her class increase in size over the year.

> When the class was small I saw the children make good progress because they were able to be given a great deal of individual attention, e.g. the children could read their books to me frequently and if a child had a problem it could be solved quickly. When the class size grew to 32 children the situation changed completely. Everything now takes much longer, the children's rate of progress is much slower than with the smaller group and the children who were progressing quite quickly have now slowed down.

Some teachers believed so strongly in the value of individual reading support for children that it was becoming a common occurrence for them to use the lunch breaks for this task.

> Not enough time to hear readers – I hear most of them at lunch time to give them some quality time.

> Obviously reading – a vital early years skill – is incredibly difficult in a large class so I now find my peaceful time to read is lunch – so I hear 6 children each lunchtime. Better but not ideal!

Teachers' comments showed several other specific manifestations of reduced individual attention.

Basic skills

Some comments specifically cited the difficulties in teaching basic skills, including reading skills, on an individual basis in large classes:

> So many early skills, e.g., letter formation, require individual guidance which is very difficult to manage within a large class.

> For the first two terms I had a small class of nineteen children . . . I was therefore able to spend more time on a one to one basis with each child. One of my first term targets is for each child to correctly form the letters of the alphabet. I feel that this target was easier to reach with a small class.

Quality time

There were a number of comments about how larger classes made it difficult to provide the quality and intensity of interactions teachers felt were necessary to adequately support children:

> Very difficult to spend quality reading time with each child.

> Last year I had a class of 24 at the beginning of the year. I found it a lot easier to give each child quality 1:1 time. In a class of 33 I feel very 'thinly spread'.

Extending reading

Another set of comments referred to the difficulty of extending children's reading in large classes:

> I like to think that my thorough planning enables me to give the children the best possible environment for learning. However this could be greatly improved if there were fewer children in the class. There would then be more time to listen to children read and work on a 1:1 basis to extend their reading strategies: comprehension of text, story making skill, vocabulary, speaking and listening skills.

Differentiation between children

The problems of reduced individual attention in larger classes are compounded when teachers seek to differentiate teaching and give individual support and feedback to every child. The more numbers increase, the more teachers appear concerned that they are not adequately catering for individual learning needs and diversity within the class.

> [In a small class] it has also meant that one to one focus areas such as reading work have been given more time, enabling the children to progress at their own rates.

> The greatest difference is in the time and quality of support that can be given to each child's particular needs. I feel that I have been able to work through problems as and when they arise, far more successfully. This has given the children a secure and settled start to school, allowing them to become independent and confident in their abilities.

> Staff have a much deeper knowledge of individual's learning needs and were able to plan, differentiate and assess work much more effectively.

Teachers were particularly concerned about not having the time to work more closely with less able readers.

> It is a constant battle to hear children read, and to hear the less-able read more often than the rest of the class.

> It is more difficult to work with individual children, specially those less able and those more able, in a larger class. The smaller the class, the easier it is to cater for the needs of all of the children.

As might be expected, concern with differentiation was seen most obviously in comments about children with special needs:

> In particular I worry about children with SEN as they cannot receive vital one to one attention for anywhere near the time they need it.

But also children with higher abilities:

> The time taken to control and encourage children with SEN is considerable. Well motivated and able children have suffered, so has the lack of individual reading.

> I think that I cannot give as much individual attention to children as I would like to. I have found that the more able children in my class are often left to their own devices – because I need to spend time with the less able.

Interestingly, a feature of some teachers' comments was their concern with children who fell between these two groups:

> Just too many children to be able to allow/encourage them to reach their full potential especially the 'middle-of the-roaders'.
>
> I believe that sometimes the children in the middle – the average achiever – may have more of a chance of being overlooked because the focus is always on the top and bottom of the scale.

Adult help

Given the difficulties of finding time to hear individuals read, it might be thought that an obvious solution would be to make use of adult help. However, some teachers commented that this was not an adequate solution.

> Hearing children read 1:1 is very difficult and I often have to rely on another adult's help, when it is available, to ensure this is done on a regular basis. I find this situation as a teacher very unsatisfactory.

I take up more fully in Chapter 7 the issue of adult help and support staff in classrooms.

Another possible solution would be to do more teaching of reading to groups of children but this was rarely mentioned as a strategy. When it was mentioned it was seen as a compromise.

> I don't find group reading very effective at this age but to hear individuals is very time consuming. I would like to spend longer with each child.

This uncertainty about the value of groups as a context for learning is a theme that emerges in various places throughout the book, and I return to this at the end of this chapter and in Chapter 9.

Results from case studies

The case studies produced a wealth of material, as it relates to the information from the previous two sections, that can be only touched on in this chapter. In line with the termly questionnaire results above, the case studies showed that teachers still relied on hearing children read as a main part of the teaching of literacy. Here we draw our effects of class size differences by selecting a few individual cases from each class size category.

Small (20 or fewer)

In one very small mixed Reception/Year 1 class, the teacher heard individual children read and worked on specific reading targets for each child. In the case of one Reception-aged child, for example, observations showed that an individual reading session focused productively on the illustrations and the differences between pictures and text. The child was then asked to tell the teacher what the story might be about by looking at the pictures. It was the teacher's belief, supported by fieldworker's observations, that this activity was extending prediction skills and contextual understandings of the text. The activity was supported by the teacher's good knowledge of each child's abilities in all areas of the curriculum and her consequent ability to target specific strategies in this way.

Despite the quantitative results, however, it does not necessarily follow that in a small class there are more sessions in which children are individually heard to read by the teacher. Observations in another small class indicated that the teacher was moving to more group-based instruction. In this small class, reading progress was monitored through reading cards although these were not used on the observation days. Individual children were, according to the class teacher, heard read by her every fortnight for about 10–15 minutes. This low frequency is surprising given the small number of children in the class. In fact, despite the small class, the teacher thought it preferable to hear the children '*As often as possible*' and remarked that she '*Would love to do it more*'. It appeared that the national literacy strategy had affected the extent of hearing individual children read. The teacher said that teachers are '*not given time to hear individual children read*'.

Small medium (21–25)

Another teacher attached great importance to reading to and with pupils, and seemed to use time with pupils effectively. Children were heard read in detail by the teacher three times a week for 5–7 minutes. She devoted about an hour each afternoon to this. Despite other children interrupting the teacher to show her their work, the field-notes indicated that this was high quality input, involving active teaching rather than passive hearing. The teacher discussed the story line and pictures, helped children blend letters, decode words, distinguish between graphically similar words (for example in the case of 'was' and 'saw' – '*close your eyes so you can see it in your head*'). She checked sight vocabulary on key words sheets, monitored phonic knowledge, changed the book with the child, and made a note in their reading folder. Work was geared to individuals: for example, teaching one boy to say 'th' rather than 'f', and to read words beginning with those letters. There was time to read the whole book.

So although there are likely to be more opportunities to hear children read in a small class, much depends on interpretation of the literacy strategy and the teacher maximizing the effectiveness of such sessions, which will include strategies to reduce interruptions.

Large medium (26–30)

One teacher placed considerable value on hearing individual children read, and it was potentially an opportunity for sustained one-to-one interactions between the teacher and child. However, it was also the time in which the teacher was likely to be interrupted by other children. While many factors are likely to influence the frequency of these interruptions, class size would seem to be important. As we saw above, in larger classes the teacher's time is spread more thinly for hearing children read, and this is aggravated if there are more children to cause such interruptions. During the summer term the teacher reported that she heard the children read individually once a week. However, she felt that twice was the ideal number.

This teacher employed several strategies in attempting to reduce such interruptions. First, she would try to make the children aware of her expectations (*'It's quiet reading time and that's what it means'*). Second, a parent would often work with a group and in the summer time they were observed circulating and assisting those children who were not part of the group a teacher was focusing on. Third, the teacher would frequently repeat and reinforce her expectations to the class. These tactics helped, but all made additional demands on the teacher, and which may not have been so pressing in a smaller class.

Large class (30 plus)

The teacher in one large class of Year 1 and Year 2 children said that she did a guided reading session once a week, in groups of 8 or 9 children. They also read individually to an adult two or three times a week. The fieldworker noted one instance when the teacher called a boy to read to her. The boy read to her for 2½ minutes at the same time as she looked around the room at the 27 other children present at the time. The teacher gave lots of praise but there were no other comments and no instruction was heard. The next child to read to her – another boy – read for 2 minutes. Again there was no instructional talk or engagement with the reading, and many interruptions from other children. Two children were then called to read to the teacher, one on each side of her, and she listened while talking to the rest of class. Overall, the teacher's main role was to check that the children actually practised reading the book at home and organize a change of book when needed. During sessions when she heard children read, her comments were encouraging but no instruction was heard.

Conclusions: class size and individual support for reading

There is a good deal of support from the quantitative results, based on teacher estimates, that as class size increases there is less time for teachers in the classroom to give individual support for reading, in the form of hearing children read.

Teachers' reports in the end of year questionnaires indicated that it was not just the amount or frequency of hearing children read but also important qualitative dimensions that suffered in large classes. These included the quality of instruction, extending reading, and meeting different individual needs, most obviously of less able children, but also more able and also children in between these two extremes. The case studies also indicated that pressures of time in larger classes could mean more interruptions and attention to individuals was more superficial, for example, just checking the correctness of words rather than a more instructional engagement with the text.

Underpinning the comments of teachers, as expressed in the end of year questionnaires, seems to be a central belief that for children of infant school age (that is, 4–7 years) individual attention is an important part of the effective teaching of reading. It is the difficulty of reconciling this belief in the need for individualization of instruction, along with the pressures exerted by contextual features like large classes, that appears to be the source of the strong sense of frustration expressed by a lot of teachers in this study (see also Moriarty et al. 2001). They felt that they were not able to provide the amount and quality of individual attention they would like, and larger classes aggravated this frustration.

As mentioned earlier in this chapter, recent developments in the UK, such as the national literacy strategy, have encouraged a more structured, less individualized, approach to the teaching of reading, at least in Y1 and Y2. It is probable that teachers' beliefs about individual support for reading have changed accordingly. However, we do know, from responses to our questionnaires (Moriarty et al. 2001), that some Reception and KS1 teachers were frustrated by some aspects of recent curriculum because they were seen to be at variance with their belief in the benefits of individualization of teaching. In the face of the demands of the literacy hour, and again perhaps aggravated by large class sizes, teachers may feel they are unable to contribute effectively to individual reading support, and may feel the effort is not worth it. The tendency to give up on hearing individual children read would therefore be understandable.

Given that increases in class size seem to be related to a decrease in hearing children read individually, what alternatives might there be for teachers in larger classes? One of the components of recent approaches to the teaching of literacy is guided group work. Again, these changes may have affected teachers' views, but it was interesting that teachers in the study rarely mentioned group work in literacy as a possible solution to problems posed by large class sizes. It is quite likely that this lack of interest reflects a continuing belief in individualization of instruction discussed earlier.

Another obvious strategy would be to make more use of support staff and extra adults. Teachers can perceive extra help in class in a positive light and no doubt value their help in hearing children read. But some teachers also believe it is ultimately their responsibility to monitor each child's progress, and make sure they are being sufficiently catered for. As we saw in Chapter 1, the UK government has recently invested resources into the provision and training of teaching assistants, and so the results in this study, which predate such moves, are in this regard out of date. However, there are still questions about the pedagogical role of teaching assistants not answered fully by recent legislation, and this will include the nature of interactions with children during individual support for reading. We return to the role of teaching assistants in Chapters 7 and 9.

How effective is the strategy of hearing children read on an individual basis as one part of the teaching of literacy? The practice can be questioned when it is not embedded in a coherent policy toward reading instruction, and when individual sessions may do little more than check in a superficial way accuracy of reading. I still have a vivid memory of a videotape shot many years ago involving a primary-aged child reading to her teacher, who, when she noticed the teacher was not listening to her but attending to another child, turned slightly to the camera, smiled in a knowing way, and deliberately started mouthing nonsense words.

But it is also important to consider the value of hearing children read on an individual basis when it is done well. The case studies indicated that teachers varied in how effectively they managed and interacted within individual sessions with children. Some teachers did little more than listen and correct, and did not offer feedback or make teaching points. In some classrooms, sessions in which children are heard to read seemed subject to interruptions, not so much because of the number of children but because strategies were not in place to minimize interruptions, or perhaps because there was an understanding that they were acceptable. There were also examples (especially in smaller classes) where individual support for reading was used in service of a clear approach to the teaching of reading, in which teachers' interventions were not just checking for accuracy but were probing and showed an instructional engagement in the child's understanding of text. This indicates that although class size will affect the extent of individual support, much will also depend on teachers considering how best to maximize, pedagogically, interactions with children when hearing them read.

The general implication of findings reported in this chapter is the need to re-evaluate the role of individual support for reading. As we have seen, there are a number of contradictory influences at work, with contextual influences, and recent legislation, at odds with at least some teachers' deeply held views about what is an appropriate approach with young children.

6 Class size and children's attentiveness and peer relations

The effect of class size on pupils can be considered conceptually in relation to academic progress, but can also be seen in a second way, in terms of social and behavioural adjustment. It might be expected that in larger classes, with more children bidding for the teacher's attention, there will be more distractions and children will be more likely to be inattentive and off-task. Relations between children may also be expected to suffer. In this chapter I examine whether these expectations are justified.

The importance of a child's early social and academic adjustment to school has been recognized in Britain for some time. Research was conducted at the end of the 1970s on factors influencing successful transition into infant and first school (for example Cleave et al. 1982) and nursery school (Blatchford et al. 1982). But a number of factors have led to a renewed interest. Recent initiatives in the UK, for example, regarding school entry assessments (or baseline assessments) have encouraged interest in more precisely assessing children's adjustment to school, soon after entry. Schools in England enter children in the year in which they become 5 years of age, and some of these children are only just 4 years old when they come into school. There are concerns about the appropriateness of existing teaching methods, class sizes and staffing in the case of such young children. Concerns with behaviour and indiscipline in schools have also heightened awareness of problems posed by some young children in school. There appear to be signs that difficult behaviour in schools is increasing. A review of research linking class size with pupil behaviour has suggested that large class sizes are at odds with a wish to improve behaviour in schools (Day et al. 1996).

One theme of several studies is that in smaller classes pupil behaviour is better and classroom management of behaviour is easier. Pate-Bain et al. (1992) report, on the basis of diary records of teachers involved in the pre-STAR research, that in smaller classes there were fewer student interruptions, and potential discipline problems were identified and solved more quickly.

Bennett (1996), in a survey of the views of teachers and others, reports that teachers believe larger classes adversely affect behaviour in class.

In this chapter we examine what our study has to say about these suggestions. Specifically, pupil behaviour in relation to class size is considered in terms of two dimensions: attentiveness in class and peer relations.

Attentiveness in class

Regardless of any connection with class size, many studies show that a key aspect related to educational achievement is attentiveness, active learning time, time on task or some equivalent term (for example Creemers 1994; Rowe 1995). It seems clear that pupils will learn to the extent that they are attentive to the topics being discussed or the work presented to them, and common sense would suggest that with more children in the class there will be more potential for distraction, and more possibility of being off-task. Cooper (1989), in his review of evidence, found several studies which showed that pupils in smaller classes attend more and spend more time on-task. Finn and Achilles (1999) have argued that the benefits of small classes are primarily in terms of increased student engagement in learning, but this conclusion is based on a follow up at grade 4 of the STAR sample (that is, after the experimental intervention had ended). They admit that further research is needed on the connection between class size and student engagement. It might also be noted that one systematic observation study did not find that pupils in smaller classes participated more in assigned tasks (Shapson et al. 1980).

There is a need to be clear about constructs used to measure attentiveness. If large classes cause children to be more distracted this could take two forms: first, an externalizing form in the sense of overtly disruptive behaviours and 'mucking about', or second, a more internalizing form in the sense of being disengaged and distracted from work. These two forms of behaviour are recognized as distinct in studies of behavioural difficulties where 'externalizing' behaviours, for example, conduct problems, hyperactive and distractible behaviour, are distinguished from 'internalizing' behaviours, such as those of an anxious-fearful nature. There is a good deal of evidence, extending over several decades, to suggest that pupils' externalizing behaviour problems, in the form of disruptive and maladjustment problems, are connected to low achievement (see Rowe 1995). As measured by Ladd and Profilet (1996), distractible/hyperactive behaviours are externalizing forms of behaviour that conceptually overlap with lack of concentration and inattentiveness in class. We hypothesized that as class size increased distractible and inattentive behaviour would also increase.

Peer relations

There is little systematic research on the effects of class size differences on peer relations, though there are suggestions that large class sizes, or large pupil–staff ratios, can adversely affect the quality of relationships between very young children. Research on children at nursery level indicates that less favourable pupil–staff ratios can lead to more negative relations between children, including more aggression, annoying and teasing (Smith et al. 1989). Smith and Connolly (1980) found that there were higher levels of aggression when there is more overcrowding in preschool settings. Other research with older pupils seems less clear; for example, Shapson et al. (1980), in a study of grade 4 and 5 children, found no difference between different sized classes in conflicts between pupils.

In considering the effects of class size on relations between children it is important to take note of the extensive literature on peer relations, stemming from developmental social psychology. While there is not space to review this work here (see Rubin et al. 1998) there is a lot of evidence to suggest that children's early social behaviour toward peers is an important predictor of later social and personal adjustment (Parker and Asher 1987). The effects of children's prosocial, withdrawn and aggressive behaviours toward peers have received most empirical support.

Prosocial behaviour is an important predictor of children's social adjustment, and has been found to relate to the development of friendships. In one study, it was reported that children in smaller classes were more appreciative of each other and showed an increased desire to assist one another (Pate-Bain et al. 1992). In the present study, it was hypothesized that as class size decreased there would be more signs of prosocial behaviours between children.

In the case of withdrawn behaviours, it is important to be clear about allied but distinct behaviours. Although withdrawn behaviour is often taken as a single dimension, on conceptual grounds different facets need to be distinguished. We can distinguish three forms: first, there are children who prefer to play alone, and can be called 'asocial'; second, children who are rejected or excluded by other children; and third, children who are wary or fearful of other children. Each of these types of withdrawn behaviour may have different origins and different relationships with later functioning.

Withdrawn behaviour might be expected to be made worse by larger classes, and it may be more difficult for teachers in larger classes to keep an eye on, and seek to draw out, children who are withdrawn, let alone find the time to distinguish between different forms of withdrawn behaviour. In line with this discussion we distinguished between three forms of withdrawn behaviour and we hypothesized that as class size increased asocial, excluded/rejected and anxious/fearful behaviours would also increase.

There is also considerable support for the importance of aggression as a factor in predicting later maladjustment (Parker and Asher 1987). Aggression in early life consistently emerges as one of the best predictors of later maladjustment, including peer rejection, delinquency, criminality, mental illness, underachievement and dropping out of school (Parker and Asher 1987; Coie and Dodge 1998).

In addition to the literature on peer relations, there is also a separate and large literature on collaborative or cooperative group work in classrooms. Again there is not space to review this here (see review in Slavin et al. 2000). Naturalistic studies of children's interactions in classrooms show that much learning in classrooms takes place in groups with other children, though many have commented that the extent of collaborative group work is limited (for example Galton et al. 1980; Tizard et al. 1988). In this study, we wanted to examine the extent to which class size differences affected peer interactive work-related behaviours. It might be expected that in larger classes teachers would be less able to monitor and control behaviour and that along with other distractions, children will engage in more social and off-task behaviours with each other. In larger classes, teachers may more easily miss squabbles between children.

The various concepts concerning children's behaviour and social relations in class are therefore complex. Measures of classroom behaviour, peer relations, and school adjustment overlap with each other and need to be conceptualized and measured carefully so that similar but different behaviours are treated separately. There is recognition that the most widely used scales need attention. Ladd and Profilet (1996) have argued that items concerning peer relations and non-peer-related items have sometimes been lumped together. Although general measures of adjustment to school have been developed (Thompson 1975), we felt that conceptualization of adjustment to school needed to take account of recent research on children's social and behavioural difficulties and research on social relationships, described above. One aim of this study, therefore, was to develop a conceptualization of, and a means of measuring, social and behavioural functioning in classrooms, including peer relations, likely to be affected by size of class.

On the basis of a review of the literature, the following aspects of classroom behaviour were investigated in relation to size of class:

1 pupil inattentiveness
2 relations between children in terms of

- asocial
- excluded
- anxious/fearful
- aggressive behaviour
- prosocial behaviour.

In line with research reviewed above, the strongest prediction was that there would be a tendency as class size increased for children to show more signs of being inattentive and off-task. We also predicted that there would be more signs of social difficulties between children as class size increased, in the form of more rejection and asocial behaviour, less prosocial behaviour, more signs of anxious behaviour, and more aggressive behaviour, though previous research does not allow firm predictions about this.

Research approach

In this chapter I concentrate on quantitative data. We have seen that previous research is limited in being relatively anecdotal and based on open-ended reported experience of individual teachers. In this chapter we combine use of systematic classroom observations and teacher ratings of child behaviour (rather than open-ended reports). As described in Chapter 2, the systematic observation data resulted in frequencies for each child of task-related and non-task-related behaviours directed at teachers, other children and when not interacting. The teacher ratings provided measures of a pupil's attentiveness and peer relations. The two forms of data collection were designed to cover allied but different aspects of attentiveness and peer relations in school.

Differences between children in large and small classes

Systematic observation results

We saw in Figure 4.2 that children in small classes were more often observed interacting with their teachers than were children in large classes. Conversely, Figure 4.2 also shows that children in large classes are more likely to interact with other children (average of 54 versus 76 observations per child) and be on their own (131 versus 154 observations).

I now look more closely at the categories describing interactions with other children. About 60 per cent of the child–child contacts were classified as task (that is, concerned with allocated work) and there were more of these in large classes. This can be seen in Figure 6.1, which shows that there are on average 46 child–child interactions about work in large classes, compared with 34 in small classes. This difference is in line with the greater amount of child–child contacts overall in large classes. There was also more than twice as much off-task behaviour with peers (more mucking about) in large classes, and this seems to reflect more than just the fact that in larger classes there was more time overall with other children. (However, this behaviour, 'mucking about', was not frequent overall.)

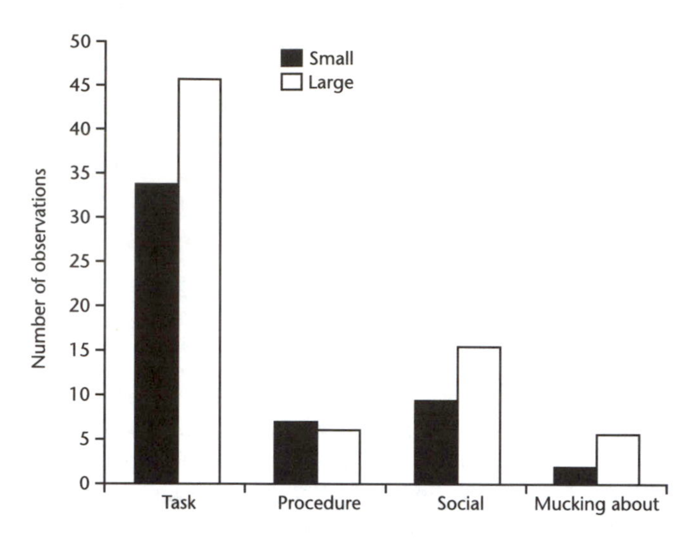

Figure 6.1 Frequency of observations in types of child–child interactions: differences between large and small classes

Apart from task-related behaviours, the most frequent category of child–child contact is social behaviours – more than 20 per cent of child–child interactions. There were significantly more social interactions in large classes. This means that in larger classes there was more likelihood of children talking with each other about matters other than work – for example, talk about outside school interests, such as television programmes, talk about each other, and so on. As described in Chapter 2, this was talk not deemed to be unacceptable to the teacher; if so it would have been coded 'off-task'. We can see in Figure 6.1 that there were on average per child 15 such interactions in large but 9 in small classes. There were no differences between large and small classes in the amount of interactions involving procedural matters, for example, talk about materials, pencils, and so on. There were very few coded instances of aggression and help between children. In summary, there were more contacts overall between children in large classes, involving task, social and off-task behaviours.

Total off-task behaviour

There were a number of behaviours in the schedule which were, by definition, deemed to be 'off-task'. There were examples of these off-task behaviours in the three social modes (that is, teacher–child, child–child and not interacting) and we can add them all up to give a total off-task score for each child. Specifically, we totalled the following behaviours: child to teacher 'inappropriate' and 'off-task', child to child 'mucking about' and 'aggressive',

Table 6.1 Frequency of observations in off-task behaviours: differences between large and small classes

	Small (average)	*Large (average)*
Child–teacher		
Inappropriate	0.9	1.4
Off-task	10.2	15.0
Child–child		
Mucking about	2.1	5.4
Aggressive	0.1	0.2
Not interacting		
Off-task (active)	3.0	6.4
Off-task (passive)	4.4	13.1
Total	20.9	41.5

and not interacting 'off-task active' and 'off-task passive' (see Table 6.1). As explained in Chapter 2, 'off-task active' was coded when the child was occupied with something other than the task in hand, while 'off-task passive' was coded when the child was disengaged during task activity, such as wandering around or daydreaming. 'Social' activities are in a sense off-task but are excluded for the purpose of this analysis because, as just explained, they were not deemed to be unacceptable to the teacher, and therefore not deliberately off-task. It is common for work-related behaviour to be accompanied by social talk. A more precise term for 'off-task' as used here might be something like 'task avoidant', though we retain the more common usage.

It can be seen in Table 6.1 that there is twice as much off-task behaviour overall in large classes in comparison to small classes (42 versus 21 observations). The most frequent forms of off-task behaviour are not attending to the teacher and not attending to their work when on their own.

Class size and the pupil behaviour rating factors

Associations between class size and total scores on the six PBR factors (that is, pupil inattentive-distractible, anxious/fearful, aggressive, asocial, excluded, prosocial behaviour) were calculated for each year.

There are two main points to make about this part of the study. First, there was some support for the connection between class size and inattentiveness in class. The association was not strong. There was no clear association at reception, but there were statistically significant but not strong relationships at Y1 and Y2. As expected the association was positive; children in larger classes tended to be more inattentive.

The second main point to make is that there was no support for the view that children in larger classes had worse peer relations than children in smaller classes. In fact, when we looked at our results closely we were surprised to find that there was a tendency for children in larger classes to be rated as less aggressive, asocial and less excluded, or, to turn this on its head, for children in smaller classes to be rated as *more* aggressive, asocial and more excluded. The results concerning the prosocial factor were not clear. Only in the Reception year is there some evidence that children in smaller classes were more prosocial.

It needs to be stressed that these results, even when statistically significant, are not strong; nevertheless they are consistent in indicating that children in the smallest classes may have the most difficulties with their peers, and that there is no evidence that classroom peer-related behaviour, in terms of aggressive, asocial and excluded behaviours, is worse in larger classes.

Conclusions: does class size affect attentiveness and relations between children?

The overall conclusions from this part of the study are as follows:

- Results from systematic observations showed that children in large classes are more likely to be off-task, particularly in terms of not attending to the teacher and not attending to their work when on their own. Results from the pupil behaviour ratings indicated a slight tendency for children in larger classes to be rated as more inattentive.
- Results from the systematic observation study showed that children in large classes are more likely to interact with their peers, and interact less with the teacher. Children in larger classes engage in more child–child task-related contacts, more social interactions and also more off-task behaviours, in the form of 'mucking about'.
- Associations between class size and factors measured in the PBR were not strong, but there was a slight though consistent tendency for worse peer relations, in terms of aggression, asocial and excluded, in the smallest classes.

The results indicate the value of using systematic observation techniques. In contrast to other forms of data collection it produces data on the basis of careful recording of ongoing behaviour (rather than, say, ratings or judgements). Although this technique has been criticized (for example Delamont and Hamilton 1986), it can be a useful research tool when answering specific research questions where data are needed on relatively easily observed, high frequency behaviours (see Croll 1986; McIntyre and Macleod 1986).

Inattentiveness and off-task behaviour

Results from the observation study and the PBR therefore suggest that children in large classes will be more distracted from work and more often off-task. This was reinforced by the qualitative data from teacher interviews and case studies (reported in Chapter 3), which indicated that pupil concentration could be adversely affected by larger class sizes.

As described earlier in this chapter, the observation and PBR data covered allied but different aspects of peer relations and attentiveness in class. That the observation measures seem more clearly related to size of class than the PBR data is perhaps not surprising. The observation measures describe moment-by-moment behaviour in classrooms, while the PBR is a retrospective rating by the teacher, and is therefore not so likely to be sensitive to immediate contextual influences. The PBR inattentiveness factor certainly involves items that reflect a lack of concentration or attention but is likely to reflect a relatively stable and enduring characteristic of an individual child. For this reason this measure may be especially useful not so much as an outcome of class size differences but as a factor to be controlled for when considering class size effects on educational progress, for example, in terms of the percentage of children in the class with attention difficulties.

There may appear to be something of a conflict between the observation and PBR results, in the sense that the PBR results suggest that negative peer relations, for example, in the form of aggressiveness are more likely in small classes, but the observation results show off-task behaviour to be more likely in large classes. However, the measures are not really tapping the same thing. We have seen that most off-task behaviour in the observation study involved not attending to the teacher or work. When off-task behaviour in child–child interactions was coded it was mostly 'mucking about' which is not the same as aggressiveness. In fact, we found that aggression between children was very rare.

Class size and peer relations

We have seen that there was no support for the view that children in smaller classes have better peer relations. Indeed the most consistent outcome was for children in the smallest classes to be rated as more likely to be aggressive, asocial and rejected. How do we explain these seemingly odd findings from the PBR?

There are two main possibilities. The first explanation is in terms of the effect of class size on teachers' perception of children in their class. One possibility is that teachers have a clearer and more visible picture of children in smaller classes. There is perhaps a tendency for children to be more salient.

As one of the research team put it: 'they're all normal until you get to know them.' Some support for this explanation comes from case studies and end of year questionnaires (reported in Chapter 4). With fewer children a teacher can get to know the children better and this would allow the teacher to be more aware of the difficulties some children might have in relating to others.

It is not possible to test this explanation exactly, which in a sense relates to the validity of the PBR, though it is unlikely to fully account for the findings. It is known that the PBR ratings do correlate reasonably well with judgements of external researchers, peer nominations and observational data on the same dimensions (Blatchford et al. 2001b), which indicates a fair degree of validity for the PBR. Ladd and Profilet (1996) also show high validity for their teacher-administered Child Behavior Scale, which is similar to the PBR. Moreover, if the experience of a smaller class increases the likelihood of a feel-good factor, with teachers less stressed (Moriarty et al. 2001), we might expect this to affect their judgements of children in a positive at least as much as a negative direction.

The second possible explanation is that the associations are saying something real about social relations in small and large classes, that is, rather than something to do with teacher's perceptions. But, if this is true, why might children in smaller classes show more of a tendency toward less social and more aggressive behaviour towards their peers? One possible explanation is found in the observation results which showed that children in larger classes spend more time with each other, interacting about work and socially, as well as 'mucking about'. Conversely, in smaller classes children interact more with their teachers. The case studies have indicated that in small classes, especially very small ones under 20, children can come to rely on the teacher, and look to them for direction, while in a larger class the children may be more likely to develop a degree of independence from the teacher, and a working and social relationship with each other. It will be remembered that in Chapter 3 we found that there was evidence of less cooperative group work in smaller classes. Certainly, some teachers felt that socially and academically there could be too few children in a class; it could mean that if children fell out, their social relations could suffer, and this might give teachers the impression that they are excluded or asocial. Using a family size analogy, it may be that in a small class the children can become overdependent on the teacher, while in a larger class children (analogous to siblings) may have to rely more on each other. In one school with a small class it was noticeable that one rather immature boy looked to the teacher for a lot of attention, which she (albeit sometimes reluctantly) gave. In a larger class she would simply not have had the time for such attention, and the boy would have been forced to look elsewhere for help. Whether this feature of small classes outweighs the academic benefits is debatable, but does suggest one potential difficulty with small classes, that teachers would need to guard against, and one way in which large classes may have unexpected positive consequences.

This second explanation remains speculative at the moment but is interesting in the light of the accepted wisdom in much of the literature of the generally positive effects of smaller classes. On the evidence so far from our class size study, small classes may be good academically for young children (see Chapter 8), but not necessarily socially.

I return to the connections between class size and peer relations in Chapter 9.

7 The role and effects of teaching assistants

As discussed in Chapter 1, one strategy for dealing with large class sizes is to make use of extra adults. Common sense would suggest that this would be helpful because it should increase opportunities for overall teaching interactions and individual support for pupils, and ultimately benefit children's educational progress. This is the basis for the UK government's recent drive to increase the number of assistants in classrooms. However, there has been little research that analyses the work that 'teaching assistants' (the term preferred by the DfES) and other helpers do in primary schools, and still less that examines in a systematic way associations between classroom support and effects on pupils' educational progress.

There is often a tacit assumption among primary teachers and parents that increasing the number of adults in a class will be beneficial to children in terms of their achievement, although the research evidence to support or refute this is relatively limited. There is currently much controversy over current plans to expand the number of teaching assistants in classrooms, with teacher associations worried that they will perform duties currently undertaken by teachers, and devalue the role of the teacher. It seems important, therefore, to examine the role and effect of assistants in classrooms.

In Chapter 8 I examine whether the presence of TAs has an effect on children's educational progress. In this chapter I examine whether the presence of classroom support influenced a number of the 'classroom processes' examined elsewhere in this book, such as the amount of time spent on teaching, time in different curriculum areas, and hearing children read. I also describe teachers' experiences of the contribution of TAs to the effectiveness of teaching and learning in the class. Finally I examine the role and contribution of TAs, on the basis of case studies in classes of varying size.

The 1998 Green Paper *Teachers: Meeting the Challenge of Change* (DfEE 1998) outlined the government's aim to increase the numbers of TAs by 20,000 full-time (or equivalent) by March 2002. Additionally, local authorities were asked to give standardized training to TAs from September 2000. There is evidence that the deployment of classroom support has expanded greatly in recent years (Swann et al. 2001).

Several research studies have profiled the typical adult other than teachers working in primary classrooms as being female, white and in her mid-thirties (Moyles with Suschitzky 1997; Lee and Mawson 1998). Lee and Mawson (1998) had 767 questionnaires returned in their study and found that there were a variety of job titles assigned to classroom support staff in schools. Some were known as 'learning support assistants', others were 'non-teaching assistants', but the most common designation was 'classroom assistants'. The variety of job titles signals the wide diversity of training/education, working conditions, contracts and pay that has been experienced by this group. However, the Green Paper (DfEE 1998) preferred to call support staff working in classrooms 'teaching assistants' claiming that this term

> captures the essential 'active ingredient' of their work; in particular, it acknowledges the contribution which well-trained and well-managed assistants can make to the teaching and learning process and to pupil achievement.
>
> (DfEE 2000: 4)

It could be argued that this is merely recognition of the work that support staff in primary classrooms have already been doing, but it implies that these adults will be expected to aid the teacher in his or her task and will themselves engage in pedagogical activities with children.

Farrell et al. (1999) found in their research in schools with TAs working with children with special educational needs, that there was a clearly understood distinction between the role of the TA and the teacher by all the stakeholders, including parents and children. The TA was perceived as being responsible for implementing programmes of work for the children, under the guidance of the teacher. However, other studies have not been able to draw such a conclusion. Mortimore et al. (1992) raised questions about the 'boundaries' between the role of the teacher and the assistant and identify two possible roles for the TA:

- *augmentation:* when the TA is involved in activities that enable the teacher to provide an enhanced curriculum
- *substitution:* when the TA has routine tasks delegated to them.

What is significant in the more recent studies is the apparent blurring of these roles. Lee and Mawson (1998) found that 77 per cent of their sample of TAs were involved in both augmentation and substitution at different times. The study by Moyles with Suschitzky (1997) had similar findings, but described a 'dilemma' between providing support for the teacher and providing support for teaching. This seems to signal a shift towards TAs engaging in pedagogic activity and not merely implementing programmes of work, which raises issues of training and education as well as status and working conditions. On the issue of roles and responsibilities, the DfEE (2000) document states:

> By definition, support for the teacher is at the heart of the role of the teaching assistant . . . The teacher plans lessons and directs learning. The teaching assistant provides support to the teacher and through this to pupils and to the teaching of the curriculum. The teaching assistant works under the direction of the teacher.
>
> (DfEE 2000: 24)

Both the Green Paper (DfEE 1998) and the DfEE (2000) document raise the profile of TAs in schools, giving them coherence as a sub-professional (or para-professional) group with training and qualifications and the recognition that schools need to change to utilize their specific skills and strengths.

> Teaching assistants are playing an increasingly important role in schools on tasks such as literacy support and helping pupils with special educational needs.
>
> (DfEE 1998: paragraph 141)

However, Moyles with Suschitzky (1997) concluded that, while TAs spent more concentrated time in supporting children's learning than classroom teachers, the pedagogic practices of TAs were often uninformed. TAs, not having been involved in the lesson planning process, were often unaware of the learning aims of a particular task or activity and therefore did not provide appropriate teaching and/or support for the children. TAs were often focused on the product of a task rather than the learning process itself and were often reactive in learning situations. Moyles with Suschitzky (1997: 3) also found that TAs were able to 'perform' like a teacher, outwardly, but were unable to conceptualize the deeper pedagogical understandings that were required for the teaching tasks they were being asked to perform. If this is true, it is hardly surprising, considering the training, education and continuing professional development required of teachers compared to that of the assistants. Despite these limitations, Moyles with Suschitsky (1997) found that TAs were often used in primary classrooms to work with the most educationally vulnerable children in lower ability groups in order to enhance their literacy and numeracy skills.

On the basis of our review of research we felt that more systematic information was needed on the role and effects of teaching assistants and other extra adults. The nature of the data collected in our study meant we were able to investigate several areas:

- Does the presence of extra staff and adults improve teaching time allocation to pupils? We examined relationships between pupil–teacher, pupil–staff and pupil–adult ratios, on the one hand, and, on the other hand, classroom teaching in terms of amount of teaching time overall, time teaching individuals, groups and the whole class; time in different curriculum areas; and the frequency and duration of hearing children read.
- How positive are teachers about their TAs? In what ways are TAs seen to contribute? We examined teachers' reports on the contribution of TAs to the effectiveness of teaching and learning in the class.
- What do TAs do in classrooms and how effectively are they used? We based conclusions on a complementary, more focused and individualized picture of the role and contribution of TAs, provided by case studies of classes varying in size.

Note: the term TA is used except when different terms are used in specific schools and in quotes from teachers.

Descriptive information on extra staff and adults

Numbers of children to teachers were very similar to the numbers of children in the class, confirming that there were few cases when classes had more than one teacher. There tended to be more additional staff and more additional hours, as class size increased for Reception and Y1, though the trend for Y2 was less clear.

When children were in Y2, it was decided in consultation with our DfES Steering Committee to collect extra information on adults working in the project classes. Information was returned on 95 Year 2 classes on a sample day during the spring term 2000. In very few classes was there no adult help at all. On average over a week there were in each class 2.6 additional adults providing 4.5 hours of additional support. There were two categories of adults in classrooms: there were 125 employed and 96 volunteer adults. Employed adults worked on average 5.9 hours per week and volunteer adults 2.7 hours.

Relevant work experience

Information was collected on the work experience of the adults working in these classes. As would be expected, employed adults had more experience than volunteer adults, who perhaps, as parents (mostly), would be more short term in their commitment. Well over half of the employed adults surveyed had more than six years' relevant experience.

Role within the classroom

Further information was also collected on the tasks and roles carried out in the classrooms.

The majority of employed staff were used in a general way in the classroom, performing the role of learning support assistant, with others supporting pupils with special educational needs. Most volunteer staff were used to perform general duties within the classroom, but most often focused on hearing individual children read.

Qualifications

Finally, information was collected on the qualifications of adults working in the classrooms. It was found that 24 per cent of employed adults and 22 per cent of volunteer adults working in these classrooms had no qualifications or training, either certificated or internal to the school or LEA. Fewer qualifications were recorded for volunteer adults, with most teachers simply describing them as 'parent', which has been included as a qualification category.

Further information on the staff in this study can be found in Blatchford et al. (2002b).

Associations between teacher, staff and adult ratios and teaching time, curriculum coverage and hearing children read

In Chapter 4 we saw that teachers with larger classes spent more time on procedural/domestic activities and less on teaching/instructional activities. It might be expected that extra support would allow teachers to spend more time teaching and relieve them of non-teaching activities. Here we therefore ask whether the presence of classroom support affected teaching time. As in Chapter 4 we used data from the termly questionnaires, in which teachers were asked to consider the period between the start of the day and the start of lunchtime on the day assigned to them. As a reminder, teachers were asked to estimate how much time, in minutes, during the designated morning, they spent in various teaching and non-teaching activities. Data were collected in the termly questionnaires. This chapter makes use of data on 279 Reception classes, 207 Year 1 classes and 118 Year 2 classes.

Associations between the pupil–teacher ratio measure and percentage teaching time for class size registered is in a similar direction to that for class size (as reported in Chapter 4), that is, as the number of children to teachers increases teaching time decreases. However, the association is lower in comparison to class size and significant only at Y1. With regard to pupil–staff and pupil–adult ratios and teaching time the only significant result is at Y2. As the number of children to adults (that is, all adults including teachers, staff and parents) increases, the time a teacher devotes to teaching decreases. These results indicate that it is class size that is most obviously related to overall teaching time, and this also largely explains the results concerning pupil–adult ratio.

As we saw in Chapter 5, as class size increases, teachers hear children read individually for less time and less frequently. This result is also found for the ratio of pupils to teachers. The association is *not* found for classroom support, however, indicating that their presence in the classroom is not being used to allow the teacher to hear children read more often (though they may be deployed to hear children read themselves).

Our results therefore show that as class sizes increase there is less time for teaching overall and for hearing children read individually. The presence of classroom support did not have a consistent or clear effect on teaching and curriculum time and none on the time a teacher had to hear children read individually.

Teachers' views about the effectiveness of classroom support in terms of teaching and learning, within KS1 classrooms

The previous section was based on relatively general quantitative measures of teaching time. Although the results indicated no obvious benefits in terms of increased teaching time, there may be other benefits revealed in subtler and less easily measured ways. In this section we ask how the teachers viewed the contribution of TAs in the classroom. To what extent did they think their presence affected the quality of teaching and learning?

We concentrate on answers to one question. Teachers were asked about the contribution of classroom support staff to teaching and learning in the class. The question invited an open-ended response. The method used to devise a coding frame by which to categorize teachers' answers was described in Chapter 2. Numbers who answered the question discussed in this section were slightly lower than those reported in Chapter 2 for the main body of questions.

First, some general trends. Almost all of the Reception, Year 1 and Year 2 classes received some form of classroom support, though the number of hours a week and quality of this support varied, as I have shown. A clear finding was that, although not explicitly asked to indicate their degree of satisfaction with the contribution of TAs to teaching and learning, many teachers spontaneously indicated how valuable their classroom support had been (50 per cent of Reception teachers, 40 per cent of Year 1 teachers (cohort 1 and cohort

2) and 32 per cent of Year 2). Year 2 teachers tended to respond with rather briefer answers, and suggested fewer general comments regarding the perceived necessity of classroom support staff than teachers of lower age groups. This may suggest that teachers of the youngest children perceive their classroom support to be more essential, for example, to help them cope with the demands of younger children.

> She [National Nursery Examination Board (NNEB) support] is invaluable, an excellent communicator with young children, and gives 100% to her job. She makes an enormous impact on the teaching and learning in the class.
>
> (Reception teacher)

> My class would not run as effectively and smoothly without good [TA] support.
>
> (Reception teacher)

The following quotes show that teachers with larger classes seemed to find extra support helpful.

> It makes a significant difference to have extra adult hands/help in the classroom.
>
> (Year 1 teacher)

> Huge and valuable. 2 minds, 2 pair of hands, 2 places at once!
>
> (Year 2 teacher)

> She was invaluable and of greatest help when I have had over 30 children in the class. Then it is vital to have another helper.
>
> (Reception teacher)

> Effective. In a class of 34 it is impossible to give the children the support they need if not supported by NNEB for at least some of the time.
>
> (Year 2 teacher)

The benefits may be particularly welcome to teachers who have classes made up of children of different age groups.

> Helps with difficulty of teaching mixed age class – makes things more manageable.

Only a very small percentage of teachers said that classroom support had not been helpful, and occasionally a hindrance, to teaching and learning, though the case studies (described below) suggest this may underestimate the true picture.

On the whole, therefore, Reception, Year 1 and Year 2 teachers saw TAs as beneficial, making a valuable contribution to the effectiveness of teaching and learning within their class. This contribution appeared to be related to their personal qualities and experience of working with young children, as well as their training.

> The quality of the work is enhanced when my assistant is with a group of children. She is very experienced and contributes very much to the effectiveness of teaching and learning.
>
> (Reception teacher)

> A classroom assistant is even better [than adult help] because they receive training about expectations in behaviour and work and the level of independence each child can achieve.
>
> (Year 1 teacher)

How teaching assistants influence teaching and learning

How more precisely do TAs influence teaching and learning in class? Table 7.1 gives a detailed breakdown of all the individual categories of answers given by teachers at each age level and a summary of average responses across the year groups, grouped on conceptual grounds into four main types:

- attention and support for children
- teacher effectiveness
- classroom management
- benefits to children: effects on learning outcomes.

Attention and support for children

As can be seen in Table 7.1, the most frequent individual response (27 per cent of teachers overall) was the view that TAs contributed through increased individual attention to pupils. When support was available, teachers felt that children received more individual help and attention, either from the assistant or themselves. Thus, individual learning needs are more likely to be met.

> The support has provided valuable one-to-one time for children who need to develop skills/ concepts. Children who need to work on the basics and children who are most able and need extending.
>
> (Reception teacher)

Table 7.1 The frequency (Freq.), percentage of teachers (%T) and percentage of overall responses (%R) by Reception, Year 1 and Year 2 teachers indicating the ways in which non-teaching staff have contributed to effective teaching and learning

		1997/98 Reception teachers (cohort 2)			*1997/98 Year 1 teachers (cohort 1)*			*1998/99 Year 1 teachers (cohort 2)*			*1998/99 Year 2 teachers (cohort 1)*			*Key Stage 1 teachers av. responses*	
Collective categories	*Individual response categories*	*Freq.*	*%T*	*%R*	*Freq.*	*%T*	*%R*	*Freq.*	*%T*	*%R*	*Freq.*	*%T*	*%R*	*Freq.*	*%T*
Attention and support for children	Increased individual attention	33	33	18	33	21	12	31	31	23	28	27	22	31	27
	Extra support for children with SEN + EBD	14	14	8	48	30	18	23	23	17	28	27	22	28	24
	Increased reading opportunities	10	10	5	15	9	6	4	4	3	2	2	2	8	7
	Vital with literacy hour support	2	2	1	11	7	4	15	15	11	14	14	11	11	9
	Reduces pressures	10	10	5	9	6	3	1	1	0.7	3	3	2	6	5
	Morale boosting	–	–	–	5	3	2	4	4	3	5	5	4	4	3
	Aid with assessments	–	–	–	2	1	8	4	4	3	1	1	0.8	2	2
	Assist with baseline assessments	3	3	2	–	–	–	–	–	–	–	–	–	1	1
Teacher effectiveness	More productive group work	30	30	16	40	25	15	20	20	15	18	17	14	27	23
	More practical lessons/activities	16	16	9	11	7	4	6	6	4	6	6	5	10	8
	More focused teaching/lesson delivery	11	11	6	16	10	6	8	8	6	3	3	2	10	8
	Planning; more time/effective	3	3	2	4	3	2	–	–	–	–	–	–	2	2
Classroom management	Delegate day-to-day duties	6	6	3	31	20	12	3	3	2	11	11	9	13	11
	Deal with practical/physical incidents	9	9	5	–	–	–	–	–	–	–	–	–	2	2
	Help with setting up activities	5	5	3	–	–	–	–	–	–	–	–	–	1	1
	Aid with discipline	–	–	–	3	2	1	2	2	1	–	–	–	1	1
	Relieve playground duty	–	–	–	3	2	1	–	–	–	–	–	–	1	1
Benefits to children	Raises standards/better progress	20	20	11	30	19	11	9	9	7	8	8	6	17	15
	Children more focused on tasks	9	9	5	5	3	2	4	4	3	1	1	0.8		
	Children less frustrated	1	1	0.5	–	–	–	–	–	–	–	–	–		

> It has provided extra support for children, to assist with their work and to give encouragement.
>
> (Year 2 teacher)

> These young children need support with personal and social development often at an individual level when first adjusting to school routine.
>
> (Reception teacher)

Classroom support, from a teacher's point of view, can be particularly valuable in the case of the youngest children in school.

Support for children with SEN

Another allied category of responses referred to support for teaching in a more specific way; for example, extra one-to-one support for children with SEN. Where classroom support is used to provide extra one-to-one support to children with SEN, teachers feel that it enables these children to make better progress educationally, their needs are more likely to be met within the class when extra support is available, and it can increase their confidence.

> Having a classroom assistant I am able to support children with special needs, either myself leading the activity or direction from the CA.
>
> (Reception teacher)

> It has been tremendous help with giving the SEN children extra input in the skills they need developing.
>
> (Year 1 teacher)

> I have a very good classroom assistant who works with the SEN group in my class. The progress made by this group, due to her excellent support, has been tremendous.
>
> (Year 2 teacher)

Support for teaching of literacy

Interestingly, in view of the results presented in the previous section, teachers also felt that classroom support can increase the time available to hear individual readers. One in ten Reception and Year 1 teachers said that individual reading support had increased. Year 1 and Year 2 teachers who completed the questionnaire a year later reported increased reading support to a lesser frequency, perhaps reflecting the decreasing role of hearing individual children read as a result of the literacy strategy.

> It also enables the children to be heard to read more often which we are convinced has a direct relation to increased reading standards.
>
> (Year 1 teacher)

> The children have been heard to read more frequently, which in all cases has helped to raise standards.
>
> (Year 1 teacher)

Classroom support is considered important by teachers as a help in successfully implementing the national literacy and national numeracy strategies. This was expressed to a greater extent by Y1 and Y2 teachers (summer term, 1999), who commented principally on the national literacy strategy. Help is needed to support literacy groups, and to provide learning support to children with SEN.

> Children with lower literacy skills (particularly writing) have had extra support which has developed their understanding of structuring and punctuating sentences.
>
> (Year 1 teacher)

> My support assistant has been invaluable this year in helping me support my SEN children during the Literacy and Numeracy Hour strategies.
>
> (Year 2 teacher)

To summarize this section so far: teachers felt that classroom support could contribute to support for learning, for example, in terms of increased individual attention for pupils, extra support for children with SEN, and increased support for the teaching of literacy through increased opportunities to hear children read and support for the national literacy strategy.

Teacher effectiveness

There were several individual responses that were more directly related to teaching, in the sense of describing instructional interactions between adults and children. The third most frequent category overall was more productive group work (23 per cent of teachers overall). Teachers felt that classroom support enabled group sizes to be smaller, and that adults could therefore more easily monitor the groups, and activities could be more structured. This in turn permits more challenging and stimulating activities, enabling children to be more focused and actively involved, and yielding more productive work and discussions. This was expressed to a higher extent by Reception teachers, and teachers who completed the questionnaire in the summer term of 1998.

Having another adult within the class means that an additional group can have teaching input.

> A non-teaching assistant can take small groups of children and provide them with the input specific to their needs.
>
> (Reception teacher)

> The children have benefited from working in small groups with an adult to support them. This has meant more of the learning has been through discussion and interaction rather than self-maintaining tasks.
>
> (Year 1 teacher)

> The children can work in a small group with adult support and therefore can produce a higher quality of work.
>
> (Year 2 teacher)

One benefit of extra help, therefore, is the part it can play in increased teaching effectiveness, though here and with other responses to the questionnaires, it is not always possible to deduce whether TAs were seen as directly providing more attention to children or whether their presence allowed teachers to give more attention to children.

There were other ways that classroom support could contribute to teaching effectiveness. One set of comments referred to practical and creative activities, particularly within reception classes. An extra pair of hands and eyes means that there is better supervision for such work, for example, in arts and crafts, design and technology, maths and language games. Given increased demands on teachers' time, some felt that creative and practical activities would be more difficult to set up without support in the class.

> Enables all children at intervals to work on activities which need to be supervised by an adult, for example art/craft activities/water capacity activities.
>
> (Year 1 teacher)

> I have a NNEB student one day a week. This is the day we do art and craft, otherwise we do very little.
>
> (Year 1 teacher)

In addition, teachers expressed the view that, as a consequence of having classroom support, they were able to be more effective in their lesson delivery and curriculum coverage. They were better able to focus upon class teaching and differentiation of work, allowing more heightened and in-depth coverage of the National Curriculum.

> A classroom assistant providing this support while the teacher continues the teaching routine enables the whole class to settle more quickly and learning to be tailored to the class needs.
>
> (Reception teacher)

> She leaves me free to extend literacy and numeracy skills of Y1 and Y2 children.
>
> (Year 1 teacher)

> Support enables objectives [and] differentiation targets to be met.
>
> (Year 1 teacher)

> Teacher able to be more focused.
>
> (Year 2 teacher)

To summarize: from the teachers' perspective, support in class can enhance effective teaching through more productive group work, more creative and practical activities, more focused teaching and lesson delivery.

Classroom management

Another set of categories indicated that classroom support can make a teacher's workload easier, that is, it assists with classroom management. Main individual responses given by more than 10 per cent of teachers at least one age level (see Table 7.1) were 'delegate day-to-day duties' and 'reduces pressure on the teacher'. Classroom support can, therefore, offer aid with day-to-day teaching-related tasks, which can lighten the teacher's workload. They can help with displays, mounting work, photocopying, or involvement with lesson preparation. Teachers said that this relieved some of the heavy burdens they felt placed upon them, allowing them to focus upon their actual teaching.

> Their assistance in displays has helped to keep the classroom instructive, stimulating and attractive.
>
> (Year 1 teacher)

> Has helped assist teacher with paperwork, filing etc – cutting down workload.
>
> (Year 2 teacher)

Benefits to children: effects on learning outcomes

The findings so far discussed show that teachers feel that the presence of classroom support can provide increased learning experiences for children, via the increased quantity and quality of adult help that children receive. Has this influenced children's learning? One in five Reception teachers and Year 1 teachers said that as a result of effective classroom support the standards of learning and progress had been raised. They reported that children show greater achievements and complete work more quickly, demonstrating an enhanced quality and pace of learning. This was mentioned to a lesser extent by Year 1 teachers (cohort 2) and Year 2 teachers (9 per cent and 8 per cent respectively).

> It would be difficult to achieve the high standards we currently have if extra supervision was unavailable.
>
> (Reception teacher)

> The support has helped to sustain the breadth of curriculum and contributed to the standard of learning the classroom.
>
> (Year 1 teacher)

> Children learn so much more with adult guidance.
>
> (Year 1 teacher)

A few teachers explicitly said that having classroom support created a more purposeful working atmosphere. The working pressure is reduced allowing the teacher to feel more relaxed and focused.

> I have more time for the children and everything is much more enjoyable, calm and productive.
>
> (Reception teacher)

Differences according to age of child

There were some indications that teachers' views on the role of classroom support varied according to the age of children and the year group taught. Y1 and Y2 teachers (more frequently than Reception teachers) said that TAs provided extra support for children with SEN. Reception teachers reported that children received increased attention. The presence of another adult allows more practical activities and lessons to take place, particularly within Reception classes. With younger children there was an increase in the percentage of teachers mentioning more productive group work and reduced working pressure. Reception teachers reported that TAs helped deal with practical or physical incidents; this was not mentioned by the older teaching age groups.

When classroom support is not helpful

A few teachers, as we have seen, expressed the opinion that their classroom support did not contribute positively to classroom teaching and learning.

> She wouldn't communicate with the children and was more of a liability, than help.
>
> (Reception teacher)

> It's about time we had trained help in the classroom!
>
> (Reception teacher)

> So much time explaining how to go about the task.
>
> (Year 1 teacher)

> Non-qualified classroom assistant requires a lot of additional input – always fighting for time to give it.
>
> (Year 2 teacher)

These comments indicate that the reasons for perceived ineffectiveness of TAs related to their direct communication with the children, as well as training and time needed to support them. We return to these areas in the section on case study results (pp. 105–18).

To summarize results in this section. From the class teachers' perspective, TAs and other adults were making a positive contribution, in terms of:

1 increased attention and support for learning

- more one-to-one attention
- support for children with SEN
- support for teaching of literacy

2 increased teaching effectiveness

- productive group work
- productive creative and practical activities
- lesson delivery and curriculum coverage

3 effective classroom management

- day-to-day teaching-related activities

4 effects on children's learning outcomes.

Case studies of the role and contribution of classroom support staff in Reception, Year 1 and Year 2 classes, varying in terms of number of children

The picture revealed by the analysis of end of year questionnaires was largely positive about the role of classroom support. However (as we shall see in Chapter 8), this picture is not consistent with the quantitative analysis of effects on children's attainment and progress. One aim of the case studies was to help understand why this difference occurred. As described in Chapter 2, the case studies were designed to provide a more detailed portrayal of individual classes, which would provide the basis for a more interpretative and grounded analysis. In this section I concentrate on teaching and learning factors connected to the deployment of classroom support.

Perhaps the most obvious point to arise out of the case studies, which can be stated at the outset, is that the classroom support varied in terms of its effectiveness in the class, and that this is probably the main reason why the quantitative analysis has not shown strong evidence of the benefits of classroom support on children's educational progress. In other words, some classroom support staff were effective and were used effectively by teachers, but some were not. In this section we take a closer look at the reasons why classroom support was effective or not, and seek to draw conclusions about its deployment in classrooms.

It is not possible to do justice to the full set of reports provided by field-workers, and in this section I provide a selective account, organized around several main themes.

Contribution of non-teaching support in terms of teaching interactions

We have seen from the questionnaire analysis that teachers could find TAs beneficial to classroom teaching, but in the case studies it was possible to explore this in more depth. There were many examples of classroom support staff working effectively, for example, with groups of children. The following extract from a fieldworker's report describes one such episode, involving a learning support assistant.

> As register was taken the LSA checked the knees of a child who had fallen in the playground and then listened as the teacher explained which children were going to be the day's 'helpers'. She assisted the teacher by finding the helpers' names to be displayed. For the next ten minutes she watched the whole class teaching session on mathematics, which she was to follow up with two groups afterwards. She then took four children who were of the same (lower) ability and of mixed gender. She first repeated the exercise of writing the

> numbers 1 to 5 on large 'Post-its' and displayed them on a whiteboard in the wrong sequence. She was interrupted twice by children working on the computer who did not know how to operate the program, but dealt with this very efficiently. When teaching the group she kept all individuals on task, drawing their attention to the order of the numbers that others were trying to correct and asking open-ended questions. One child slid down in his seat and stretched back, appearing to lose concentration, but she was quick to notice this and brought him back into the discussion. The LSA used the same strategies of reinforcing counting 1+1 as the teacher, and helped reinforce this concept. Children were then asked to write their own numbers on smaller Post-its to place in sequence in their maths books. As each child worked she checked that their number formation was correct and asked children to tell her the number they were writing. She was very patient when children who had finished alerted her to this fact and asked them to wait a moment. The quality of interaction she engaged in with individual children was high, for example, asking children to point to numbers with 1:1 correspondence as they counted, and asking them which number came before, after or next. This 'reinforcement' group seemed to gain confidence by her use of praise and worked for a period of twenty minutes on the topic.

This is a fairly typical exchange that will be found in many classrooms, but this should not blind us to the way in which the adult is effective in supporting learning. To itemize just the main features:

- she deals smoothly with a potential disruption from one child while maintaining the flow of the topic
- she keeps attention focused on the main mathematical concept that she wishes to consolidate
- she uses practical activities and materials effectively to support learning
- she offers immediate and relevant feedback on their work
- she supports them with praise and encouragement
- additionally, she complements and supports the teacher's introduction and teaching aims (not least because she had watched the teacher closely and then deliberately modelled her actions).

Let us look at another example. The adult helpers in this class were used with groups of children, and this was laid out in the teacher's lesson plans. Their direct teaching qualities were valued by the teacher, but in this class, interestingly, it was parents who provided it, not the TA. Parents helped with groups for information technology (IT), art/craft and topic activities. The teacher noted that they took the initiative in preparing materials for use with groups, such as preparations for art activities and bringing materials into the school. She felt that they were effective in establishing good relations with the children, and observations of interactions with pupils suggested that they extended pupils' learning. The observer's report described the careful preparation by two parents for Christmas craft group activities and interactions with the children in which appropriate questioning and explanations facilitated learning. It was also observed that individuals were challenged with hands-on experiences; for example, one child initially used her rolling pin to push rather than roll out her icing and was encouraged to watch carefully as one of the parents illustrated the action. The child then succeeded with this new skill. The expertise and enthusiasm of one parent for IT was especially noteworthy. This parent had set up facilities for email for each child, shown them how to access the Internet, and spent three hours a week helping children in pairs. The teacher felt that she would not have been able to set this up without this parent's initiative and expertise. In addition to the direct contribution of these parents, the successful group work they engaged in enabled the teacher to concentrate on other groups and individuals.

To summarize so far, some of the direct interaction qualities that appeared to be effective, whether by TA or parent were: questioning and explanation strategies matched to children's abilities, initiative in preparation, teaching through demonstration, appropriateness of feedback, not allowing potentially disruptive behaviour to interrupt attention to a task, and expertise in particular areas.

What of those adults who were seen as not effective? There was an instructive contrast provided by the TA in the same class as that just described. In contrast, the TA was described as 'inflexible' in her instructional interactions with children. She helped each morning for a total of seven hours a week. The teacher felt that she had a 'fixed pattern' of interactions with children that was somewhat didactic and lacking in warmth. It was felt that the TA saw her role as a disciplinarian rather than one in which she 'worked with the children'; the teacher found it difficult to encourage her to adopt a more personal and friendly style with children. As a consequence, while the TA assisted with individuals in groups, the teacher felt that she could not let her work with a group as independently as some parents were naturally able to do. As well as using very limited praise or warmth with the children, she did not extend their thinking or their creativity. This was seen in the observer's report of the TA helping with a group working on worksheets involving the placing of positions as dots on a grid. The TA's comments focused on correctness, for example, '*What are these funny dots here? These should be on lines and not in gaps*', followed by the TA rubbing out the child's dots. There were no probing or questioning techniques to enable the child to understand how far she had succeeded and why she had been mistaken.

Another case study showed limitations in direct teaching input by a classroom helper. The observer reported that the helper appeared to view her presence as a source of dissuasion. In one episode the helper was with a girl/boy pair working on the computer. The helper told the observer she did not know the program they were using and would watch to see what the children had to do. When the observer returned five minutes later the same boy was in control of the mouse. Another girl asked if she could have a go but the boy did not allow her a turn. The helper did not intervene and said afterwards that this was not her job. The program involved language and literacy work, a spelling game of CVC (consonant, vowel, consonant) words, and finding words with the same initial letter or objects whose names rhymed, for example, 'find something that rhymes with "ram" = "ham"'. The helper did not assist the boy in succeeding at this work, and he clicked at random on the screen. When asked afterwards about her role at the computer she was defensive about her non-intervention. It was the observer's view that she lacked confidence. The classroom teacher was not seen to supervise her.

As a way of summarizing reports where helpers were not effective the following features seemed to apply:

- inflexible and didactic
- role seen as dealing with the correctness of work and behaviour
- limited warmth and praise
- little probing or questioning or efforts to help children understand why they might be mistaken
- little knowledge of the task undertaken by the children
- little effort to ensure equal opportunities for all.

Another case study report provided insights into ways of viewing the contribution of TAs to teaching and learning. In this class there were two TAs, one of whom was considered to be excellent; she had worked with the teacher for many years and they got on well. She was able to work independently of the teacher and this was seen as a great asset. She was used largely to hear children read on a one-to-one basis, and to go over their weekly words. She also worked with small groups on literacy activities that had been planned and discussed with the teacher at the beginning of the lesson. The second TA was perceived by the teacher as quite capable but needed more support and this could sometimes prove difficult, for example, if she needed to discuss something with the teacher when the teacher was talking to the children. This was observed to take valuable teaching time away from the teacher.

In another case study of a Reception class, the teacher articulated the difference between her role and that of two part-time ancillary assistants

(AA). She planned for the two AAs to focus on one group only, while she planned to use her time to focus on one group but also monitor the work in the other groups (usually three). Another case study of a class provided further information on ways in which the teacher's and two TA's interactions with children differed. The teacher concentrated her time with groups working on literacy tasks, and on hearing children read individually. In the afternoon she focused on helping the summer-born children in their adjustment to school. The assistance provided by the TAs seemed valuable. They were observed preparing, distributing and tidying resources, collecting and filing children's completed work, and helping children dress after physical education. They also supported curriculum aims more directly. They gave the children a great deal of praise, enhancing their motivation. Comments included: *'He's got a lovely crown – that angel'*, of a child's picture, and *'That's really lovely, John, be careful'*. The TAs provided feedback, which mostly took the form of error correction. Other comments included, *'I want you to stop now'* and *'That's a bit too much'* (during art activity). This kind of corrective feedback was also observed when the TAs heard individual children read. It was described by the observer as taking the form of 'guided practice' and it might be contrasted with the teacher's interactions with children in the same situation, which showed more evidence of further development of skills and 'metacognitive' understanding. For example, TA1 encouraged the children in their decoding, drawing their attention to each word at a time, whereas the teacher left more space for the child to practise self-regulation, and questioning was used to encourage the child's inferences about the text. In contrast, the TAs were rarely seen questioning the children about their work.

Both TA1 and TA2 supported children's learning by modelling procedures for them, such as how to use a tube of 'glitter-glue'. Both also helped the children by, for example, warning them about taking home their Christmas cards too early. They were observed making direct suggestions to the children in both art and a literacy activity, although the latter was seen only when the teacher was interrupted by another adult, and unable to help herself.

In summary these case studies indicate that TAs had a valuable role in classroom learning, in terms of their educational interactions with children, but roles were different from those of the teacher.

In another case study of a Reception class with 24 children the teacher had two full-time assistants (a nursery nurse (NN) and a learning support assistant) shared between the two Reception classes, taking it in turns to work both classes (so that there was the equivalent of one full-time assistant in each class). Both were experienced and worked well together and with the teacher, but the fieldworker's report identified a central uncertainty at the heart of their role. They were often deployed to work with groups of children but the researcher noted that they saw their role as primarily to prepare resources, to tidy areas of the classroom, to take and manage groups and individuals so that the class teacher could concentrate on teaching. Although the NN and LSA did encourage pupils to think, more often they tended to give children answers or tell them what to do. They rarely showed that their interactions with children were informed by consideration of appropriate pedagogical practice. At no time during the visit were they seen to consult the class teacher's plans. In summary, the observer noted that the NN and LSA were both competent, but that there was an ambiguity and uncertainty about their role when it came to 'teaching' situations with children.

There is much more that could be offered by way of accounts from the fieldworkers' reports but perhaps enough has been offered to raise questions about the appropriate role of teaching assistants when it comes to direct interactions with children. I return to this theme at the end of this section.

Classroom support is affected by its reliability and consistency

The case studies made it clear that the expected benefits from classroom support could suffer if there were uncertainties about the regularity and predictability of their presence. In one case, voluntary help included two mothers who came for 40 minutes each week to read with groups of children. They were reliable and much appreciated by the teacher. In contrast a man from a local company also came to hear readers once a week, but the teacher found this less useful as there was no feedback and no time to discuss with him what he should be doing.

Some teachers felt that part-time support was not always helpful, because it made planning more difficult and children were less able to benefit from their presence. In one class a TA's time had been cut and another TA had been introduced for a few hours in the class and in the school office. The teacher felt that one full-time assistant would be more beneficial than splitting the hours between two people because the children could then build up a firmer relationship, and feel comfortable approaching them with questions. The teacher felt that uncertainties caused by the TAs' changing hours and days were not conducive to developing expectations about whom to approach when the teacher was busy with other children. It was observed that some of the younger children, who attended on a part-time basis, and who might be most likely to need help, were particularly unsure about the TAs' roles and did not feel confident in approaching them. The teacher felt that if the children had begun the school year with the teacher and TA working in conjunction throughout the week, this problem might have been more easily overcome.

One theme to emerge from the case studies was therefore the importance of reliability and consistency in classroom support, for example, with regard to hours worked. If support was unpredictable it could be disruptive and, from at least some teacher's point of view, better to have no help at all. Another main theme concerns the preference on balance for a given amount of time for support to be used to employ one person rather than spread it between more than one person.

Contribution of classroom support is affected by care in planning

We have just seen that difficulties can arise as a result of the hours TAs are employed and spend in class. Teachers may have little control over this. But the case studies also provided evidence of ways in which the time TAs were present was not always used effectively. One teacher explained that her class was small in comparison to previous years and therefore made teaching and monitoring easier. However, at this stage in the Reception year class routines were still being established and the teacher found it difficult to teach a small group intensively without being interrupted. During the first morning observation there were two TAs and one parent helper present in the classroom. Despite the high ratio of adults to children, the teacher was still not free to work alone with a small group. At no time during the observation did the teacher instruct the children to approach the TAs if they had a problem with their individual work. The teacher was very conscious of one child identified as having behavioural problems who demanded a lot of her attention. It was observed many times during the day that the child would disrupt teaching. Although there was usually a TA present, the teacher always dealt with his problems herself. It was the observer's conclusion that encouraging the TA to spend more time with the child would have helped the teacher spend more time with the rest of the class.

This case study suggested that it was not only the class size, or the amount of classroom support, which affected the effectiveness of teaching in the class but also the use of adult helpers' time. Making it clear to children and helpers that children should approach helpers rather than the teacher at certain times would have eased many problems.

In some classes the teacher had in place a written document that was used by the TA and other classroom support for guidance about what to do next. In one Reception class, the teacher wrote the learning objectives of activities to be done with the children in a book, which the TAs could consult to clarify their role that day. The teacher said she did this because although one TA was effective and independent, the other TA and parent helpers needed a great deal of direction, which she could not give once the lesson had begun. In another class an educational care officer (who had no particular special needs qualifications) worked with individuals for three hours a week. She was well organized and was seen working with children with SEN, getting their folders and following the targets set down in the documents. Planning with the teacher was done through these records.

Planning in these cases is therefore done through a shared written version of the objectives of learning tasks, as well as suggested activities. This would seem helpful as a reminder in cases where TAs are already competent and familiar with the class. In cases where TAs need more guidance and support, it is certainly better than them waiting for the teacher, for example, when she is too busy with children, but it would not seem a sufficient system on its own.

A case study of one Reception class showed how the teacher planned the lesson and activities then shared her learning intentions with her two part-time and long-standing AAs. She characterized her relationships with the AAs as cooperative rather than 'hierarchical', and any imbalance in their roles was to do with responsibility rather than authority. She described the quality of relationship between her and the AAs as important and dependent on good communication and the AAs feeling valued. This teacher was wary of using parent helpers in the first term of the school year as she felt it could prevent the children from settling into school.

The amount of time that teachers could spend supporting TAs was a theme to emerge from the case studies. This was particularly evident when TAs attached to the same class differed in the support required. In one Reception class the teacher reported having a good relationship with all her adult helpers. She felt that she always gave them explicit instructions of what she wanted them to do, but one of the classroom assistants needed more guidance and direction than the other. She usually had to be shown, by example, exactly what she was required to do. The teacher found it frustrating when she had to spend so much time instructing the assistant because she could have completed the task in the same time herself. By contrast the other assistant was more self-motivated and confident. All of the paid classroom assistants in the school had a weekly meeting with teaching staff to discuss any issues or problems that had arisen, but this did not seem to deal with the teachers' frustration.

In another school there were two TAs, one in the morning and one in the afternoon. One therefore focused on literacy and numeracy, because these areas formed the mainstay of the morning's work, while one concentrated on the less formal activities that predominated in the afternoon. In this sense deployment of support was different in terms of curriculum, but this simply resulted from the time they were employed to work.

Case studies showed that more support does not necessarily mean more effective support, even when the staff involved are individually effective. In one case study of a large class there were different TAs each week. There was 15 hours' support a week. During the observation week there were six different TAs used for 5 hours on literacy, 5 hours on maths, 2 hours every Wednesday for end-of-KS1 Stage test practice, 2 hours every Friday afternoon for listening to individual readers, 1 hour for a special needs TA, who usually took a group of Y2 children. In addition there was a parent used for 2 hours on Monday afternoons for science, and a student on postgraduate final teaching practice. The adults concerned were described as excellent; the observer actually made a wrong assumption that one was a teacher. They attended a lunchtime weekly KS1 planning session and were given the weekly written plan so they should know which group of children they were working with and a basic outline of the task, before arriving in the classroom. But the teacher felt that planning with so many different adults was difficult and she did not have enough time to talk through tasks in much detail. Observations indicated that much planning took place in the classroom when the TA arrived. The teacher tried to arrange things so that a particular TA would continue a task with different groups of children, for example a grammar task from the literacy hour. But the lack of preparation could be a hindrance to effective teaching. On one occasion when a TA was working with a group in the annex room during the daily mathematics lesson, it was felt by the observer that opportunities to maximize child learning were missed, as the TA was not prepared for the session. Instead of setting up practical tasks or games, which would have been a logical next step, the children were just given worksheets and pages from books to complete. In a large class the teacher has to rely on the classroom support, and the quality of their input depends on the teacher's ability and time to plan appropriate activities that the classroom support can use. It did not appear that in this class the potential of classroom support was realized.

The complexity of arrangements involving classroom support in some classes was evident in another case study of a mixed aged class (15 Reception and 15 Y1 children). During the visit there were a total of eight adults seen working with just the Reception children in this class. Apart from the class teacher there was a primary helper with a specialist teacher assistant (STAR) qualification, who had also attended SEN courses and who worked mainly with individual statemented children concentrating on language and literacy work, a classroom assistant who trained as an NNEB 29 years ago, another classroom assistant who had a history degree and a career in the civil service and who now had a job share with the NNEB, three volunteers (parents) and the head teacher, who took all the children for one session. All had a good deal of experience and worked well together and with the children. The job share arrangement seemed to work particularly well, with the two women having an obvious respect for each other and their joint contribution to the children in the class. However, the observer concluded on the basis of her detailed observations that there was a large amount of 'dead' time, when voluntary helpers in particular were sitting and listening to other adults interacting with the children. It seemed that the management and the role of classroom support needed attention, particularly with regard to supporting children. It was also felt that in this class, and given the numbers of adults, plans for the sessions could be shared in written form to avoid the need for verbal communication which could interrupt teaching time. There was also a case made for more opportunity for feedback and evaluation so that opinions could be shown to be valued and used in the context of professional development of knowledge and understanding.

The role of training

While it may seem obvious that effective use of classroom support will depend on training, there are a number of difficult issues. In one case study of a Reception class, the teacher said that the ancillary had probably received '*at most, 2 days' training*', but she was not confident that further training would change her authoritarian style. She reported that she was not able to pre-plan lesson objectives with her. She commented that the ancillary doubled as a 'dinner lady' supervisor which she felt *'probably did not help her classroom role'* and emphasized her authoritarian/non-social role. The observations in class confirmed the teacher's impression – the ancillary adopted an authoritarian and detached approach referred to by the teacher.

In another case study of a Reception class, the teacher had worked hard with her two ancillary assistants to translate in a coherent way lesson plans and learning aims. As we saw above she placed a lot of emphasis on the quality of her relationship and communication with the AAs. She considered that the ideal AA would have had a good deal of experience with young children, a desire for hard work and a genuine liking of children, and she saw this as more important than any specific training. She felt that since working with her one of her AAs had '*come on a lot*'. This AA had studied modules in child development at diploma level but the teacher did not think this had shown itself in any overt way in her work.

In another case study the use of a LSA resulted in a better quality of work than if groups of children had been asked to work independently. Individuals achieved the learning objectives by working with a teacher substitute, even though she was untrained for this work. Her pedagogic practices may have been uninformed but as we saw above she modelled herself on the class teacher. By having copies of lesson plans beforehand she was aware of the learning aims, but she was conscious in a broad and informed sense of the process that she had to cover as well as the product. She also worked with both lower and upper ability children for mathematics tasks. This indicates that written guidelines supported by discussion with the teacher, modelling of teaching strategies and perhaps a natural ability to relate to children can contribute to effective support for learning. It also indicates that training may well be important, but it is the implementation of this training in specific classroom learning contexts that is crucial to children's learning and this will depend on the lead set by the teacher and efforts to ensure teaching and curricular aims are understood by classroom support staff.

Another indication of the importance of the personal qualities of classroom support, over and above any training they may have received, is provided in the contrast between the LSA just described and another LSA in a parallel class. This LSA worked on routine and cross-curricular tasks. Although in contrast well qualified, her impact on children's learning appeared not so great as the other LSA. It must be said that she did provide a valuable input: she eased the load of resource preparation and supervision of children. Her understanding of the reading scheme seemed adequate. She provided pastoral care when children needed it, and her presence reduced the day-to-day pressure on the teacher of dealing with 26 young children. But in terms of direct teaching input she was not as effective.

One head teacher explained that the TAs, as far as she knew, had no training. After arriving at the school she had changed the TA monitoring system and now held weekly meetings to discuss how the TAs' time had been spent and encouraged evaluation of this time. She hoped that this would lead to maximizing the benefit the teacher and children received from having extra help. She also reported that the TAs now went on various courses to train them to deal with specific needs, for example, autistic children, and children with reading difficulties.

In one school, support was to varying degrees seen to be inactive during the time that they were observed. It was not the status of support that affected how well they were used or the way they were used, but more their lack of comprehension of the role they could play. Though untrained, these adults were observed to work in ways such as watching children and intervening when it looked as if disagreements between children might disrupt the calm of the classroom. It was the observer's judgement that all three women in this class would benefit from training and briefing about their role in supporting both the class teacher and the children.

The case studies suggested aspects that it would be useful to cover in training. One observer felt that this applied to the teaching of literacy in Reception, particularly phonics. The support she provided for children when hearing them read was not sufficient.

The composition of the class, for example, in terms of characteristics of the children, can affect the relevance of training of adult support. In one class there were many children considered to have special needs. The school funded classroom support for just four hours a week and this was the same for each class, regardless of the number of SEN children. The teacher found this inadequate, especially as the previous year she apparently had many more hours' support for her class. It was felt that the less able children suffered, for example, because adult help during group work was not available. The support included an educational care officer (ECO), and an NNEB qualified helper for one hour a week. One child observed had difficulties at home and at school. The teacher knew about this in detail and was able to respond sympathetically, but due to lack of support his educational needs were not being met. The child of average ability who was observed also had difficulties as he lacked confidence in his work and socially. He was having a particularly bad day when the observer was there and the teacher was able to sit next to him and talk to him quietly keeping him on-task throughout the afternoon. This may not have been possible with more children in the class. It can be deduced that with effective help in the class the needs of the other children would also be met, and a TA could have sat with the child, thus freeing the teacher to interact with other children.

In a case study visit in July 2000 (Reception class of 29 children) the issue of training for learning support assistants in the school was high on the agenda. The LSA who worked with the Reception class had been hired many years ago and saw her job as primarily one of carrying out 'maintenance' jobs around the classroom to help the teacher. She was happy with the job and was clear that she was not a trained teacher and had no desire to be one. However, given the staffing costs involved for the school, there was pressure from the head teacher for the LSAs to be doing more in the classrooms of an academic nature. The LSA was wary of the training course she had been asked to go on. It was the teacher's judgement that the course had had little effect on the way that the LSAs in the school interacted with children. They were not perceived to ask children educationally appropriate questions and did not go into work in enough detail with children. The teacher felt that the LSAs were still too inflexible with children.

Conclusions from case studies

There are several themes, arising out of the case studies, which bear on effectiveness in the use of classroom support staff.

One theme to emerge from the case studies was the importance of reliability and consistency in classroom support. There were problems when support was not planned for and was fragmented; for example, when a teacher was not sure who would be with her class, or when she had several people for short lengths of time. Teachers could spend valuable time supporting staff, or opportunities were lost. There was preference, on balance, for a given amount of time for support to be used to employ one person rather than spread it between several.

Another theme was the need for careful planning – how the teacher used the staff and helpers available to her. Case studies showed that it was not only the amount of classroom support that affected the effectiveness of teaching in the class, but also the way in which it was used. There were enough examples given to show that more support does not necessarily mean more effective support, even when the staff involved are individually effective. The beneficial effect of communication between the teacher and TAs, for example, about lesson plans, was discussed, as well as the use of written notes for quick reference by assistants.

There were implications for training. There was the salutary conclusion that the personal qualities of adults were a major factor in the effectiveness of their contribution and this was over and above training. There is also the general point that, in order for training to be effective, whatever the qualities and merits of individual courses, it would need to be integrated into classroom practice and connect with a teacher's aims and lesson plans, and take account of the often deeply held views of TAs about their role and contribution. One feature of case studies was the potentially important role of teachers' modelling of concepts, to be followed up by TAs. Overall, training will need to attend to pedagogy and direct teaching.

So perhaps the overriding theme arising out of the case studies concerns the contribution of classroom support in terms of teaching interactions. The unavoidable conclusion from the case studies is that support staff *will* be involved in direct teaching interactions and that it is therefore necessary to consider how these can work well. What is the appropriate role of TAs when it comes to direct teaching? It is important to be clearer about this issue because it lies at the heart of the teacher union worries about the growth in numbers of TAs. In general, we argue that it would be helpful to consider what kinds of pedagogical models might be helpful as a way of positioning the pedagogical role of TAs and teachers. One model, constructed by Arends (1994), involves three teaching functions: executive, interactive and organizational. It could be argued that, while teachers perform all three functions, TAs are engaged with the interactive function alone, and therefore need education and training in order to be able to carry out this role effectively. Another general model is Shulman's (1986) account of domains of knowledge (content knowledge, pedagogical knowledge, knowledge of learners, general pedagogical knowledge, knowledge of educational contexts, curriculum knowledge, knowledge of educational ends). Presumably teachers should be knowledgeable in all domains, but what are the appropriate domains of knowledge for TAs? Creemers' (1994) basic model of effective characteristics of teacher behaviour might be used. This is based on a thorough review of the literature on effective teaching, and covers areas such as structuring the content, clarity of presentation, questioning, immediate exercises, evaluation, feedback and corrective instruction.

These and other models could be used to consider what the appropriate role of TAs might be when it comes to direct teaching. This raises general but fundamental questions about effectiveness in teaching interactions and pedagogy and it seems likely that one cannot separate views about the deployment of classroom support staff from views about effective pedagogy. More specific questions that arise out of this discussion include: should they be expected to cover all aspects? What level of pedagogical knowledge should be expected, and how general or domain-specific should it be (for example, connected to particular responsibilities in the classroom)? Finally a general distinction has been been made by some between 'experts' and 'novices', with TAs seen as 'novice' teachers rather than 'experts'. However, while this may be a valid theoretical position to take for teachers, it is questionable when applied to TAs who have not had similar training and education to teachers and who, unlike teachers, have not been socialized into the profession.

We also need to raise questions about the *contexts* within which classroom support may be used most effectively; for example, small group work, where they can concentrate their contribution within a wider pedagogical and curriculum context set by the teacher. One worrying finding identified in recent research on within-class groups in primary schools (Kutnick et al. 2002) is for TAs to work with lower achievers – and sometimes this means small groups of boys or individual boys. Existing guidance on training for TAs is mostly concerned with subject knowledge in numeracy and literacy and management aspects of work. Pedagogical coverage is limited and implicit and left to the mentor at schools to model and discuss with the TAs. The effective TA should be able to extend thinking and develop skills, understanding and metacognitive processes in children. This will require even *more* complex skills if the children that TAs are working with are the lower achieving groups in primary classrooms. These aspects, then, need to be addressed in any training/professional development designed for TAs.

The role of teaching assistant: what can we conclude?

Analysis of connections between the three ratio measures (and class size) and three sets of classroom processes – teaching time, curriculum time and hearing children read – showed that the presence of classroom support did not have a consistent or clear effect on teaching and curriculum time and none on the time a teacher had to hear children read individually.

Some teachers felt that classroom support staff were helpful in hearing children read, though the termly questionnaire data indicated that it had not helped teachers devote more time to hearing children read. There is a widespread expectation that parents will have a main role in hearing children read at home, though not that they will be able to substitute for teachers. Again (as reported in Chapter 5), we detect a good deal of uncertainty about the role of individual support for reading and a need to clarify more deliberately its contribution and the role of different adults – teachers, TAs, volunteer help and parents at home – with regard to it.

The results from the analysis of teachers' end of year comments showed that from the class teachers' perspective, TAs and other adults were making a positive contribution, in terms of increased attention and support for learning (more one-to-one attention; support for children with SEN; support for teaching of literacy); increased teaching effectiveness (productive group work; productive creative and practical activities; lesson delivery and curriculum coverage); effective classroom management and effects on children's learning outcomes.

How do we reconcile the seemingly different picture about the contribution of TAs and other adults arising from the end of year questionnaires – which were broadly positive – and the numerical results concerning relations with teaching time (reported in this chapter) and from the main statistical analyses of relations with children's academic progress (to be reported in Chapter 9) which were less clear? The case studies were helpful here. Perhaps the most obvious point to arise out of the case studies was that the support in classes varied in terms of its effectiveness, and that this is probably the main reason why the quantitative analyses did not show clear evidence of the benefits of classroom support on children's educational progress. In other words, some classroom support staff were effective and were used effectively by teachers, but some were not. In the section reporting on the case studies we took a closer look at the ways in which, and the reasons why, staff were effective or not, in terms of four main areas.

Several themes emerged from the case studies: the importance of reliability and consistency in classroom support, the need for careful planning, and implications for training. But the main conclusion was that classroom support staff will inevitably be involved in direct teaching interactions and that it is therefore necessary to consider what kind of contribution is appropriate. Despite advances in training for TAs, there is still more that could be done to consider the role of classroom support staff, not just in general terms relating to appropriate parts of the curriculum or general expectations about, for example, support with group work, but also in terms of the moment-by-moment interactions with children, as well as the pedagogical knowledge that underpins such interactions. There is a need to articulate more deliberately what kinds of pedagogy are relevant, in the case of TAs, and to use this to inform training. Overall, we conclude that one cannot separate views about the deployment of TAs and other adults from views about effective pedagogy. It was suggested that models of pedagogical knowledge and classroom teaching be examined and developed to help position the contributions of teachers and TAs, and help inform support and training for TAs. It may be that we need to consider TAs and teachers in much the same terms when it comes to teaching interactions but that, as we have seen in the case studies, teachers have responsibility for other dimensions, for example, the executive and organizational aspects, which sets them apart. Considering teachers and TAs together on one dimension does not therefore devalue in any way the teachers' contribution, but it might help to clarify the contribution of teaching assistants.

8 Class size and educational progress

In previous chapters I have examined connections between class size and several classroom processes – within-class groups, teaching and pupil concentration and peer relations. In this chapter I turn to the main statistical analysis and ask whether class size is related to pupils' educational progress. As we saw in Chapter 1 this has been examined in previous research though results are not always clear-cut. We also saw that our study was designed to provide a more sophisticated examination of connections between class size differences and educational progress. It was designed to allow analysis of connections between class size and progress, across the whole range of class size differences, not just comparisons of selected class sizes. It provided an assessment of whether class size effects varied according to the attainments of children, and it controlled for variables that might possibly affect the relationship between class size and attainment. In this chapter we also examine the role that the classroom processes, examined in earlier chapters, have on the connection between class size and children's achievements. This chapter is concerned only with quantitative analyses and includes only those variables entered into quantitative analysis. It does not therefore include qualitative data on classroom processes, reported in earlier chapters. It is also selective in terms of the quantitative process variables it includes. In Chapter 9, results from the quantitative analysis reported in this chapter will be integrated with the qualitative results presented earlier in order to arrive at a full account of the effects of class size.

It is our view that the analyses reported in this chapter are some of the most sophisticated yet undertaken on this topic. However, there is a difficulty when writing a book meant for non-statisticians in that it is not possible or desirable to explain in any detail the statistical approach that has been used or the results. It is important though to understand the basic approach and I shall try to describe this in an accessible way. The interested reader is encouraged to follow up the references below which will provide a comprehensive explanation of the methods used and analyses conducted, as well as a full description of results.

This chapter is also selective in another way. A full listing of results would be too long and indigestible. My aim in this chapter, therefore, is to explain in more detail those results which I feel are the most significant and interesting.

Finally, I must say how indebted I am to Paul Bassett for the statistical analysis on which this chapter is based.

Approach

The effect of class size upon progress was examined for each of the three years separately (that is, Reception, Year 1 and Year 2). The analysis of the data for each year followed the same pattern. Initially, the effect of class size upon attainment was examined. In other words the association was calculated between class size and the children's attainment scores at the end of the school year. However, it is important to control for children's attainments at the beginning of the year to be sure that these are not affecting the relationship between class size and end of year attainment. One reason for this is because attainment at the end of the school year is strongly related to attainment at the beginning of the year, and the relationship between class size and attainment could be distorted if some classes have pupils with higher abilities than others. The association between class size and end of year attainment was therefore calculated again, this time controlling for pupils' attainment scores in previous years. An important point to make is that results from this type of analysis show us whether class size is related to children's *progress* over the year. This is a main advantage of a longitudinal research design. It is more powerful than examining relationships with attainment at one point in time, and is more indicative of whether (though it cannot prove that) class size is causally related to progress.

To gain further insight into whether class size effects are the same for children of all abilities we also looked at the results in a third way by examining the relationship between class size and children's progress for children who started the year with different levels of attainment. Specifically, we divided the children into three groups based on their scores in literacy and maths at the beginning of the year – those in the lowest 25 per cent, those in the middle 50 per cent and those in the highest 25 per cent of test scores.

The next step was to examine the effect of factors that could potentially affect the relationship between class size and progress. We therefore controlled for characteristics of pupils (such as term of entry, eligibility for free school meals, age), class characteristics (such as the percentage of children in the class eligible for free school meals, the percentage of children in the class with behaviour difficulties) and teacher characteristics (such as teacher experience and professional training and qualifications).

The effects of class size in the reception year on progress in later years was examined, and also whether changes in class size from one year to another affected later attainment.

Lastly, we examined relationships between class size and key process variables, relationships between these process variables and children's progress, and then whether these process variables appeared to mediate or explain the class size effect on progress. Remember, this chapter is just concerned with selected quantitative measures so this analysis is only a partial assessment of the relationships between class size and classroom processes.

For reference, a full list of the variables used in these analyses can be found in Table 8.1.

Table 8.1 Summary of variables included in the statistical analysis

Variable	*Description*
Basic variables	
Class size	Average registered class size over all three terms of the year
Literacy	Attainment at baseline, and the end of Reception, Year 1, Year 2
Mathematics	Attainment at baseline, and the end of Reception, Year 1, Year 2
Ability group	Based upon test score at beginning of year, divided into low (25%), middle (50%) and high (25%)
Pupil characteristics	
Term of entry	Entered school in autumn term (78%) or the spring/summer terms
Free school meals	Whether entitled to free school meals (17% yes)
Age	Age at 1 September 1996 (measured in months)
Ethnic group	Ethnic group defined as white (91%) or non-white
Nursery attendance	Had pupil attended a nursery (46% yes)
English first language	English as a first language (98% yes)
Special needs	Whether the child was classed as special needs (5% yes)
Gender	Was the child male or female (51% male)
Class characteristics	
% free school meals	% of class entitled to free school meals
Deviation from class mean	Difference in attainment from class mean at beginning of year
% aggressive pupils	% of pupils in the class defined as aggressive
% hyperactive pupils	% of pupils in the class defined as hyperactive
Variability in class	The range of abilities in the class, measured by standard deviation

% above 1 σ	% of pupils above 1sd of class average
% below 1 σ	% of pupils below 1sd of the class mean
Mixed age class	Whether there were pupils from more than one year in the class
Classroom size	Size of the classroom (measured in m^2)
Extra adults	Number of extra adults present on average in the classroom
Teacher characteristics	
Teacher age	Age of the teacher categorized as <30, 31–40, 41–50, 51+ years
Teacher experience	Number of years of teaching experience
School experience	Number of years at the current school
Non-contact time	Average amount of non-contact time per pupil per week
Self concept	How the head-teacher rates teaching ability (high or low)
Reading training	Whether the teacher has received training in teaching reading
Language training	Whether the teacher has received training in teaching language
Maths training	Whether the teacher has received training in teaching maths
Class changes	
Change in class size	Change in the registered number of pupils from the previous year
Class movement	Did pupils move up year groups in the same class, move contrary to their classmates, or split into different destination classes?
Process variables	
Number times heard read	Number of times each child was heard to read each week
Length time heard read	Length of time each child was heard to read each week
Percentage teaching time	The percentage of school time spent teaching the whole class
Asocial behaviour	In the highest 20% of pupils on asocial scale
Excluded behaviour	In the highest 20% of pupils on excluded scale
Aggressive behaviour	In the highest 20% of pupils on aggressive scale
Hyperactive behaviour	In the highest 20% of pupils on hyperactive/distractible scale
Number of groups	The number of within-class groups
Size of groups	Average size of within-class groups
Teacher stress	Self-perceived teacher stress (divided equally into high/low groups)
Teacher satisfaction	Self-perceived teacher satisfaction (divided equally into high/low groups)
Teacher self concept	Self-perceived teacher stress (divided equally into high/low groups)

It might be helpful to give a bit more detail to the measures we used. Pupil attainment in literacy and mathematics during the various years of the study was measured on a number of standard tests, each of which was made up of a number of different components. Different tests were measured on different scales, which makes it difficult to compare between them. For consistency, all measures were, therefore, transformed into a single standard scale. Without getting into the technical details, the basic idea is that the average test score is set at zero, and one unit of the scale represents one standard deviation. This is a standard statistical unit, and is approximately equivalent to the difference between a pupil at the class average and a pupil in the top 20 per cent of the class.

In order to provide a clear expression of these results, in this chapter I present them in graphical form. In these graphs attainment is displayed on the vertical axis and class size on the horizontal axis. The attainment scale is expressed in standard units as just described and will vary from a positive number (more than average) to a negative number (less than average). The higher the score, the higher the pupil achievement. Class size in these graphs is simply the number of children in the class. One advantage of this way of presenting results is that relationships between class size and attainment can be easily interpreted, and I shall describe in more detail how to do this when we look at the first graph.

Another advantage of this type of scale is that it is easier to contrast the results with other studies, as many other researchers have also used this approach. Results expressed in standard deviation units are the same as what has become known as an 'effect size' and which is sometimes used to express how strong a relationship has been found. This is a much more precise guide to how strong the relationship is than just whether or not it is statistically significant.

All analyses were performed using statistical regression methods. These methods allow the exact relationship between class size and attainment to be determined. It is also possible to use these methods to take into account, or 'control for', the other factors that might influence pupils' attainment (that is, the child, class and teacher characteristics in Table 8.1).

The analyses also allowed for the multilevel structure of the data. As I have said, this is necessary because we cannot assume that children's scores on tests and other measures are independent of each other; it is known that results from pupils within the same class and school tend to be more alike than results from pupils in differing classes and different schools. Three-level models were therefore used: (1) pupils nested within (2) classes, which were in turn nested within (3) schools.

Just one more point about the statistical analysis needs to be made. Again, without describing the technical details involved, the analysis allowed an accurate examination of relationships between class size across the range of the distribution of class sizes. One problem with simpler regression approaches (technically those restricted to plotting linear or quadratic relationships) is that the relationships indicated in the graphs are less accurate, for example, because they are affected by data at the extremes. To provide a more exact estimate a more advanced modelling technique was used taking into account the exact relationship across the range of class sizes. This is an important point but one that is difficult to express in everyday language. For those wishing to get a full understanding of how we conducted these analyses, and results in full, see Blatchford et al. (2002a) and Blatchford et al. (in preparation).

Reception year: literacy

Let us look first at results for the Reception year. The effect of class size upon literacy attainment is shown in Figure 8.1.

The sloping line on the graph is called a 'regression' line and it is this that tells us about the relationship between the two variables. In this graph there are clear signs of a relationship between class size and literacy attainment. We see that as class size increases the literacy scores of children tend to decrease, or, to express this the other way round, as class size decreases in number children tend to do better in literacy. This was highly statistically significant. One of the advantages of expressing results in graphical form is that we can compare the effects of different class size sizes. If, for example, we

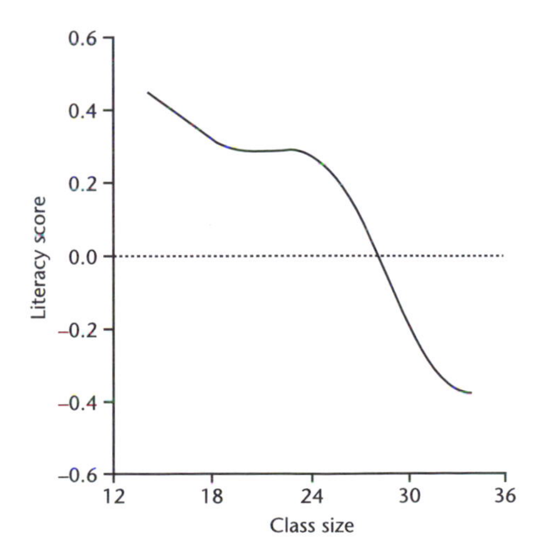

Figure 8.1 Relationship between class size and literacy attainment: Reception year

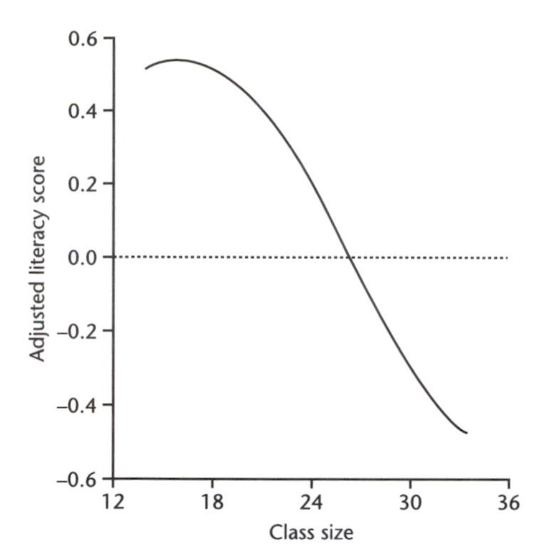

Figure 8.2 Relationship between class size and literacy attainment adjusted for baseline attainment: Reception year

compare a class size of 30 with a class size of 20, the graph tells us that there is a difference in literacy scores of about 0.5 of a standard deviation. The reader can see this by drawing vertical lines up from 30 and 20 on the class size axis, to where they meet the 'regression' line on the graph, and then drawing two horizontal lines from these two points across to the literacy scores axis. The difference between these two points – in this case $-0.2 + 0.3 = 0.5$ – tells us the difference in literacy scores between the two class sizes.

I have already shown why this simple analysis needs now to be extended to take account of attainments at the beginning of the school years, that is, by including the pre-Reception year scores in both literacy and mathematics. The 'adjusted' relationship between class size and literacy is shown in Figure 8.2.

After adjusting for the pre-Reception year scores, there was still found to be a highly significant effect of class size upon the literacy scores. Indeed, the effect is stronger. If we compare a class size of 30 with one of 20 we now find a difference of about 0.7 of a standard deviation.

Does the effect of class size vary between attainment groups?

To answer this question, the pupils were split into three attainment groups, based on their pre-Reception year literacy scores. The lowest attaining 25 per cent of children were put into one group, the middle 50 per cent of pupils were entered into a second group, and the top 25 per cent were put into a third group. We then looked at the relationship between class size and literacy attainment (controlling for pre-Reception scores) for each of these three groups separately.

The results are shown in Figure 8.3, and are very interesting. The relationship for the three groups is almost identical for class sizes over 25. The relationship flattens out somewhat for classes with less than 25 pupils in the high and middle baseline groups, but the literacy scores continue to increase at a constant rate for smaller class sizes in the low baseline group. This means that decreases in classes below 25 continue to have a positive effect on literacy progress for the initially lowest attaining group, but less so for the middle and high attaining groups. (Although the relationship between class size and progress varied between the groups, it was still statistically significant for all three ability groups.) The effect of a decrease in class size for the lowest attaining group can be judged by comparing literacy scores for a class size of 25 with those of a class size of 15. Reading across to the difference in literacy scores (as described above) shows the difference to be about 0.8 of a standard deviation. This is a very large difference.

Looking very briefly at the effect of pupil characteristics (see Table 8.1 for a list of these) on progress we found that there was a significant effect of first language not English, gender, special needs and term of entry upon literacy progress, while there was also slight evidence of an effect of free school meals. There was found to be no evidence of an effect of ethnic group, age or nursery attendance.

There was no evidence that any of the teacher characteristics (see Table 8.1) have a significant influence upon progress in literacy.

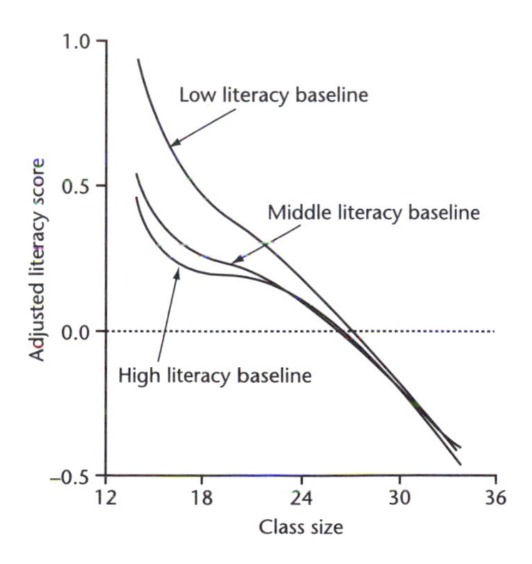

Figure 8.3 Relationship between class size and literacy attainment by ability group: Reception year

Final, summary analysis of class size and literacy: Reception year

In order to get an overall picture of the effect of all variables, including class size, on literacy progress over the Reception year, all potentially important variables were entered into a single analysis. This is particularly helpful in order to take into account possible overlap between variables related to attainment. The variables now related in a positive way to progress were English not the first language, and in a negative direction spring/summer school entry and special needs status. There was also a negative effect of male gender and eligibility for free school meals, which were of borderline statistical significance. Importantly, there was still a clear class size effect and there was still a significant interaction between attainment group and class size, such that the relationship between class size and progress varied for the three attainment groups.

The final relationship between class size and progress, that is, after all the other variables significantly related to progress are included, is less strong than that shown in Figure 8.2, that is, when just the relationship between class size and progress are considered. This can mostly be explained by the fact that pupils entering school in the spring or summer term perform less well at the end of Reception year compared to those entering school in the autumn term. These later entrants were generally found in slightly larger classes than the autumn entrants.

Reception Year: mathematics

We conducted the same set of analyses, this time examining the relationship between class size and the end of Reception year maths scores. This is shown in Figure 8.4.

There is a clear relationship between class size and maths attainment. Children's attainment decreased as class size increased.

We then controlled for pre-Reception (baseline) attainment scores in both mathematics and literacy, so that the effects of class size were more representative of the progress made during the course of the year. The revised relationship is shown in Figure 8.5.

It can be seen that after this additional adjustment there is a highly significant decrease in mathematics attainment with increased class size. Again comparing class sizes of 20 and 30 we found a difference of about 0.7 of a standard deviation, and as with literacy this is a large difference.

We then examined the effect of class size separately for the three different attainment groups, with the pupils split into three groups based upon the baseline mathematics results. This time there was no evidence of an inter-

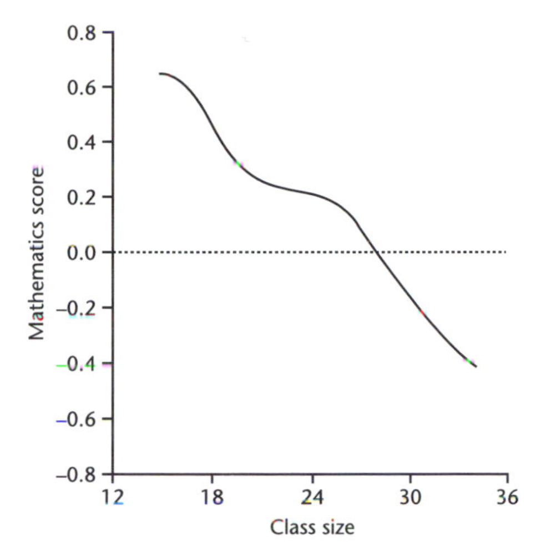

Figure 8.4 Relationship between class size and mathematics attainment: Reception year

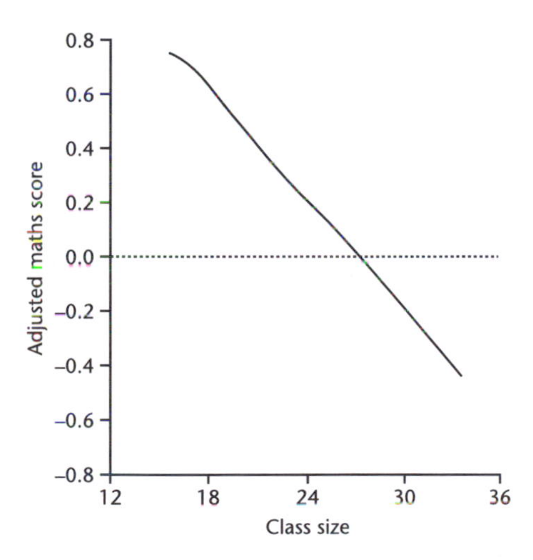

Figure 8.5 Relationship between class size and mathematics attainment adjusted for baseline attainment: Reception year

action between class size and attainment group. In other words, in the case of maths there is no evidence that class size has a different effect according to a child's level of attainment.

This result is illustrated in Figure 8.6, where it can be seen that all three groups have approximately parallel lines.

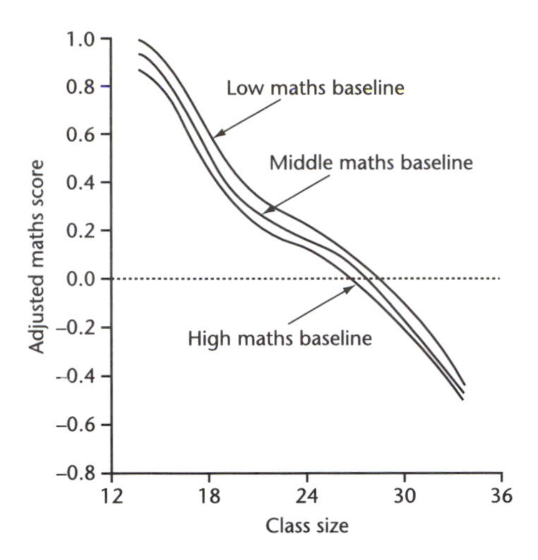

Figure 8.6 Relationship between class size and mathematics attainment by ability group: Reception year

Looking very briefly at the effect of pupil characteristics on attainment, we found there was a highly significant effect of free school meals, ethnic group, age, first language not English, special needs status and term of entry on the maths results. There was no evidence of an effect of nursery attendance and gender upon mathematics progress over the Reception year.

As with literacy, there was no evidence of a significant effect of any of the teacher variables upon progress in mathematics, nor that any of the variables had a significant interaction with class size.

Final summary analysis of the effect of class size on mathematics progress: Reception year

Once again a final analysis was conducted with all the variables significantly related to maths progress included, along with class size. This analysis showed there to be a significant positive effect on mathematics progress of English not being the first language, increased age, and deviation above the class mean, while there was a negative effect upon progress of spring/summer school entry, entitlement to free school meals and special needs status.

As with literacy, class size and mathematics progress were still related, and the result was highly significant. The effect is smaller after additional adjustments for the potential confounding factors. Again this is mainly attributable to the term of entry variable as spring/summer entrants are found in slightly larger classes than autumn entrants.

Year 1 and Year 2: literacy and mathematics

The same set of analyses were conducted at both Year 1 and Year 2 for both literacy and mathematics. In summary, the connections between class size and children's educational progress were less clear. There was some suggestion of a relationship between class size and literacy during Year 1. The 'unadjusted' effect of Year 1 class size upon the Year 1 literacy results was examined initially, and is shown in Figure 8.7.

It can be seen that there is little sign of a relationship between class size and literacy score for the majority of the class size range. There are signs of an increase in attainment for very small classes, below about 23 children, but there were not many classes of this size, and this is why there is little evidence for an overall effect.

Children's attainment results from previous years were then included so that the effects of the Year 1 class size upon the progress made during the year could be more accurately assessed. The literacy and mathematics scores at both the end and beginning of the Reception year are included. The 'adjusted' relationship between class size and progress in literacy over Year 1 is shown in Figure 8.8.

There are still signs, though reduced, of an effect of smaller class sizes, but the overall shape of the relationship is relatively unchanged. There was still found to be no overall effect of class size.

In the case of maths in Year 1 and both literacy and maths in Year 2, overall there was little evidence that class size was related to differences in

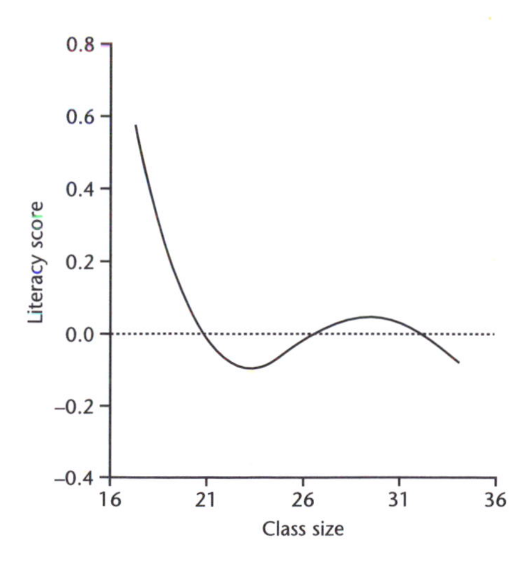

Figure 8.7 Relationship between class size and literacy attainment: Year 1

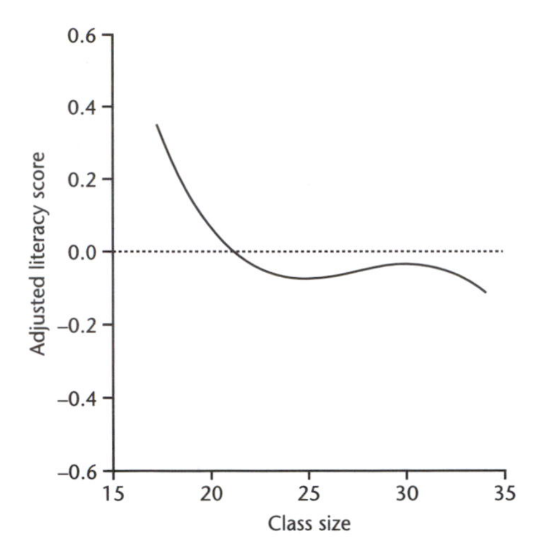

Figure 8.8 Relationship between class size and literacy attainment adjusted for previous attainment: Year 1

children's educational progress. For this reason I do not present these results here. The interested reader can find them in Blatchford, Bassett, Goldstein and Martin (in preparation).

We can therefore conclude that the effect of class size on children's educational progress is marked in the first year of school, but is not so clear in the second and third year of school.

The effect of Reception year class size upon Year 1 results: literacy

We now need to examine whether the benefits gained by small classes in the reception year are still evident at the end of Year 1. Figure 8.9 shows the relationship between Reception year class size and Year 1 literacy scores. Results were adjusted for previous test results, that is the pre-Reception year attainment in literacy and mathematics were added. The effects of class size shown in Figure 8.9 now more accurately reflect the progress made during the first two years of school. We can see that there is still found to be a negative relationship between the two variables (as class size goes up, progress goes down), which was again found to be highly statistically significant.

The results of the analysis also indicated that this time there was no evidence of an interaction between class size and attainment group, in other words, no evidence that the effect of Reception year class size upon Year 1 literacy attainment was different for pupils of differing start-of-school attainments.

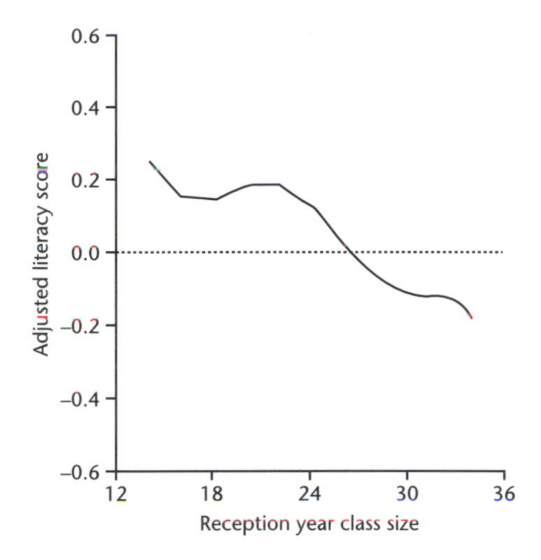

Figure 8.9 Relationship between Reception year class size and literacy attainment adjusted for baseline attainment: Year 1

In the final analysis, that is, including all variables significantly related to end of Year 1 literacy, it was found that the relationship between class size in the Reception year and literacy attainment at the end of Year 1 was still evident. We can conclude, therefore, that the gains made by being in small Reception year classes are still evident at the end of Year 1. However, the effect of small classes is reduced from that observed over just the Reception year. Again the inclusion of the term of entry variable in the analysis tends to reduce the class size effect. As discussed previously, those pupils entering school in the spring or summer terms were entered into slightly larger classes. This explains why the class size effect is reduced when adjusted for this variable.

The effect of Reception year class size on Year 1: mathematics

The same methods were used to assess the effect of Reception year class size on Year 1 mathematics attainment. When pre-Reception literacy and mathematics attainment scores were added, the relationship between class size and mathematics score was as shown in Figure 8.10.

The overall relationship is statistically significant. There still appears to be a negative relationship between the two variables for larger class sizes, but there appears to be little relationship between the variables for smaller class sizes. More specifically, children make more progress in maths as class sizes decreased to about 23, but thereafter there was no effect.

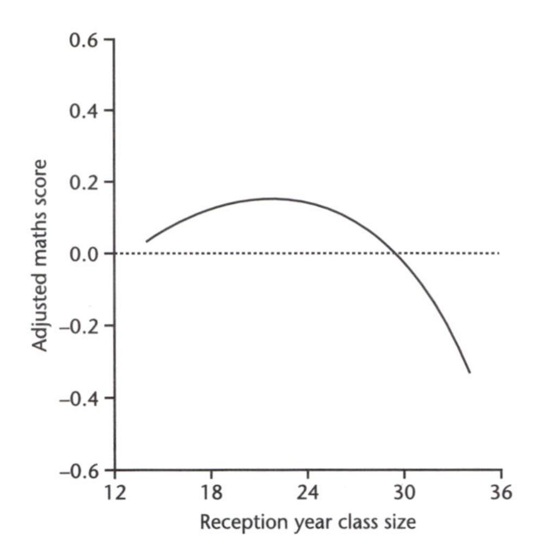

Figure 8.10 Relationship between Reception year class size and mathematics attainment adjusted for previous test scores: Year 1

In the final analysis, that is, including all variables significantly related to end of Year 1 mathematics, it was found that the relationship between class size in the Reception year and maths attainment at the end of Year 1 was not evident. Therefore it can be concluded that the gains in maths progress made by being in small Reception year classes appear not to carry through to the end of Year 1. As with previous results, the change in the relationship between the two variables is mainly attributable to the inclusion of term of entry.

The effect of Reception year class size on Year 2 results: literacy

There is therefore some evidence that the gains made by being in small classes in the Reception year are still evident at the end of Year 1 in literacy. Does this effect of the Reception year class size continue to the end of Year 2? Again, the pre-Reception literacy and mathematics scores were added in order to allow for the prior attainment of the pupils. The adjusted relationship is shown in Figure 8.11.

It can be seen that there is a decrease in attainment with class size for classes up to 30, after which there was found to be an increase in achievement. There was found to be no overall evidence of an overall effect of class size upon attainment. Therefore, the gains made in literacy during the Reception year are not clearly evident by the end of Year 2.

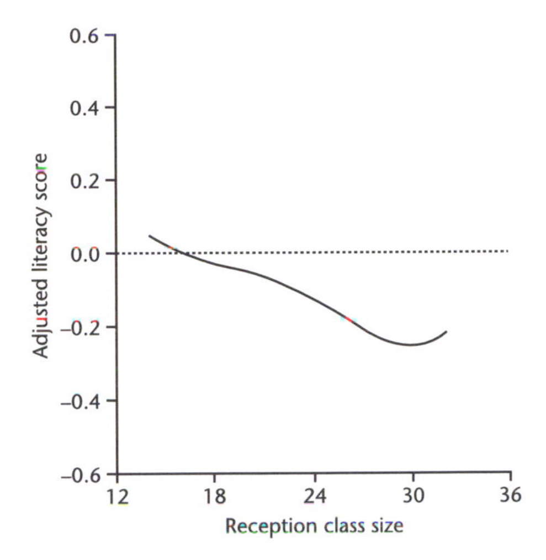

Figure 8.11 Relationship between Reception year class size and literacy attainment adjusted for previous test scores: Year 2

The effect of Reception year class size on Year 2 results: mathematics

In the case of maths, the relationship between class size in the Reception year and attainment at the end of Year 2 is significant but appears to be quite irregular with no obvious trends between the two variables.

The effect of movement between Reception and Year 1 classes on educational progress

In our analyses we were able to look at the effect on educational progress of changes in class sizes between the Reception year and Year 1. These results were interesting. There was found to be a significant effect of both the change in class size from Reception and the type of movement of pupils upon the progress in literacy during Year 1.

To be more specific: those children who moved differently to the majority of their class made, on average, 0.31 units less progress than pupils who moved to the next year as a group. The relationship between the change in class size and progress is shown in Figure 8.12. It can be seen that pupils moving to a larger class tend to make less progress than those who remain in similar sized classes (as the number of 'extra' children in the class goes up, academic progress goes down). So, for example, a child who moved into a class with eight

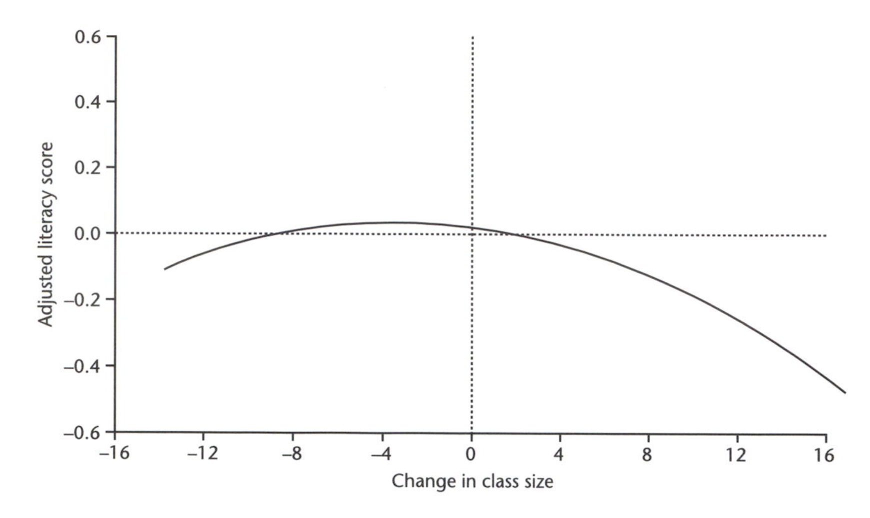

Figure 8.12 Relationship between change in class size from the Reception year and progress in literacy during Year 1

more children made about 0.2 standard deviations less progress than a child who stayed in a class with the same number of children (indicated on the graph by 0).

These results indicate what might be called a 'disruption' effect when moving from Reception to Year 1 into a different sized class, which is magnified when the class is bigger.

There was no evidence that the type of movement between different classes had any effect on progress in mathematics. However, as in literacy, there was found to be strong evidence that the change in class size from the Reception year had an influence upon progress. The relationship between change in class size on progress is shown in Figure 8.13.

As with literacy, it can be seen that pupils make less progress in maths when moved to a different sized class between Reception and Year 1, especially when moved to larger classes.

The effect of staff and adults, in addition to the teacher, on children's educational progress

As well as the effect of class size, the effect of additional staff and additional adults on pupils' educational progress in maths and literacy was examined. The results can be easily summarized. There was no evidence for any year for either literacy or maths that additional staff or additional adults in the class

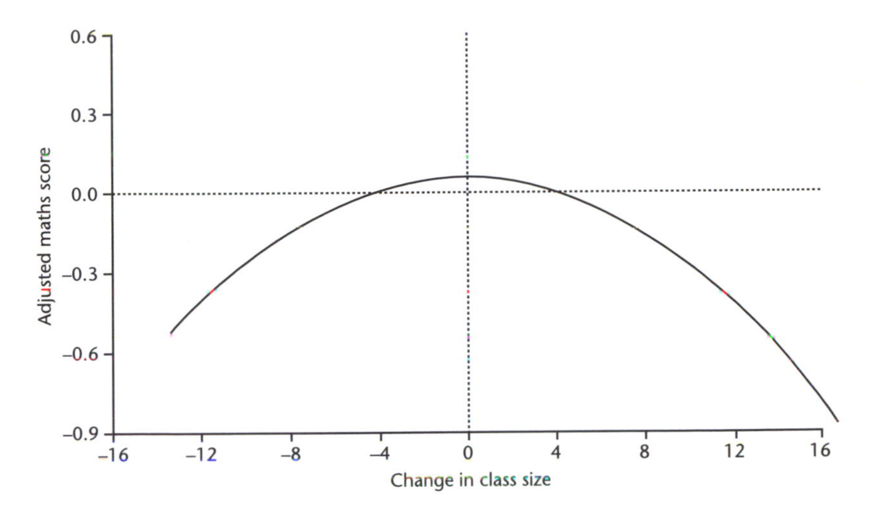

Figure 8.13 Relationship between change in class size from the Reception year and progress in mathematics during Year 1

had an effect on children's progress and they did not interact with class size, indicating that there is no apparent 'compensation' effect of having extra adults in the class.

Class size and classroom process variables

The last step in the analysis was to include classroom process variables. There were 12 process variables selected from those used in previous chapters. They are listed in Table 8.1. If a process variable is to explain or mediate the class size effect, it is necessary for it to be related to both attainment and class size. We therefore examined the relationship between the process variables and both of these two factors (that is, class size and attainment separately). This seemed to us the basic first step in establishing associations between class size, classroom processes, and achievement, needed before any further causal modelling was justified.

The relationships between class size and classroom processes has, of course, been examined in previous chapters. As I said earlier, in this chapter we look at only a selection of just the quantitative process variables. Because of the more sophisticated multilevel statistical analysis used there is slightly less likelihood of results showing up as significant, especially if the individual relationship with class size is not statistically strong, even though still statistically significant. For this reason fewer variables are identified as being statistically related to class size.

Given that the clearest connection between class size and progress has concerned the Reception year I concentrate on results for this year.

Reception year

Literacy

For class size and process variables, the results tended to confirm those in previous chapters. There was a significant effect of class size on the number of groups, the percentage teaching time and the number of times children were heard to read.

For process variables and literacy attainment, the results showed that progress in literacy over the Reception year is influenced by the number of times the children are heard to read, percentage teaching time and the aggressive and inattentive/hyperactive behaviour variables. Increased teaching time and the number of times the children are heard to read are both positively associated with progress. Pupils with aggressive behaviour make 0.08 units less progress than those without, while inattentive pupils make 0.21 units less progress.

When class size (analysed separately for each attainment group) is included in the analysis the same variables were found to be significant, but the effect of the number of times the children are heard read is reduced. The effect sizes for all other variables are almost unchanged.

The behaviour variables are not strongly related to class size, so it is not surprising that the effects of these variables are unchanged by the inclusion of class size in the model. The effect of percentage teaching time is unchanged although this is related to class size. The number of times children were heard to read was also found to be related to class size, which explains why the effect size is reduced after being adjusted for class size.

The significant variables were entered into a single analysis with and without class size in the model. When class size was left out there was found to be a significant effect on progress of inattentive behaviour, percentage teaching time and the number of times the children were heard to read. There was not found to be an effect on any of the other behaviour variables after these additional adjustments.

With class size added there was a significant effect of inattentive behaviour and percentage teaching time upon progress, but no evidence of an effect of number of times the children were heard to read.

The relationship between class size and literacy progress was calculated after taking into account the significant process variables. There is little difference in the relationship between class size and attainment from that observed before the process variables were added. This means that the class size effect cannot be easily or obviously 'explained' by the process variables.

Mathematics

The same methods of analysis were applied to the mathematics scores. Excluded, aggressive and hyperactive behaviour variables were found to be strongly related to progress, and in each case pupils with worse behaviour make less progress. The behaviour variables were found to be unrelated to class size, and therefore their influence on progress is unaffected by the additional adjustment for class size.

There was also found to be a significant effect of percentage teaching time and number of times the children are heard to read when class size was not included in the model. Those that were heard to read more, made more progress, while an increase in teaching time led to an increase in progress. Both of these variables were still found to have a significant effect on progress when adjusted for class size, even though both are related to class size.

All significant variables were subsequently entered into a single analysis. The results indicated that when class size was not included, there was a significant effect of the number of times children were heard to read, percentage teaching time and inattentive behaviour. All the behaviour variables are strongly related to each other, so after adjustment for inattentive behaviour, there was no additional effect of the remaining variables.

When the procedure was repeated with class size in the model, the same three variables were found to be significant. The effect size of each variable is similar to those observed in the individual analyses.

The relationship between class size and maths progress is similar even after the process variables were added to the model. Therefore it appears that the attainment benefit gained by pupils in smaller classes are not, in this statistical analysis at least, explained by the classroom process variables.

Year 1

Given that class size and progress were not clearly related in Year 1 and Year 2, it is not sensible to examine the mediating role of the process variables. However, for information I briefly summarize relationships detected by these analyses between class size and the process variables, and relationships between the process variables and progress.

For class size and process variables, the number of groups increased with class size. Percentage teaching time was greatest for the smallest classes.

For effects on literacy attainment, progress in literacy was influenced by pupils' aggressive and inattentive behaviour. Pupils with aggressive behaviour and inattentive behaviour made less progress.

The second stage of the analysis was to enter both significant variables into a single model. There was found to be no effect of aggressive behaviour when adjusted for hyperactive behaviour, as these two variables are strongly correlated.

Mathematics

The same analyses were performed for the mathematics score. The analysis indicated that the length of time the children were heard to read and all four behaviour variables were found to influence mathematics attainment. Pupils who were heard to read for more than 10 minutes per week, made 0.27 units more progress than those who were heard to read for less time. Pupils with disruptive behaviour characteristics made less progress than those without.

The significant process variables were entered into a single regression model, and only the statistically significant variables were retained. The results of this procedure indicated that after the additional adjustments, only inattentive behaviour and the length of time that the children were heard to read were found to influence attainment.

Year 2

For class size and process variables, the results indicate that there is a significant effect of class size upon the occurrence of aggressive behaviour. As indicated in Chapter 6, the occurrence of aggressive behaviour decreases with increased class size, which is the opposite of what might be expected.

For effects on literacy attainment, the results indicate that when class size is not included both aggressive and inattentive behaviour were found to influence progress in literacy. There was also slight evidence of an effect of excluded behaviour. Inattentive pupils made 0.35 units less progress than those who were not, while pupils with aggressive behaviour made 0.26 units less progress. When class size is included the same variables were found to be significant, and the effect sizes were very similar. The two significant process variables were entered into a single model and there was found to be a significant effect of both aggressive and inattentive behaviour upon progress in literacy.

For class size and mathematics, the results indicate that when class size is not included there is a highly significant effect of hyperactive behaviour upon progress in mathematics, with hyperactive pupils making 0.32 units less progress than non-hyperactive ones. There was found to be a significant effect of both inattentive behaviour and the number of groups when class size was included. When entered in a single regression model, both variables were found to be statistically significant.

Conclusions

Here I briefly review the main results from this chapter. I shall discuss their implications for policy and practice in Chapter 9.

There was found to be a significant effect of class size upon progress in both literacy and mathematics during the Reception year, after adjusting for potentially confounding factors. The benefit of small classes on literacy progress was most evident in lower ability pupils, with the effect not so evident in the higher attainers. The benefit was constant for all ability groups in mathematics.

One of the best known projects in the area, the Tennessee STAR, found that decreasing class size from a medium to small class (equivalent to a reduction of 7 pupils) resulted in an average increase in attainment of 0.16 units for maths and 0.17 units for literacy. This effect size is comparable with the results found from the analysis. For an equivalent change of 7 pupils (in the class size range of 20–30) the effect size for literacy attainment was approximately 0.29 units for the low attainers, 0.20 units for the middle attainment group and 0.15 units for the high attainers. For mathematics the equivalent figure was approximately 0.17 units for all ability groups. The figures from the STAR study are only indirectly comparable with the results from our study because class sizes were smaller and the environment in which the study was performed was different.

Progress in both literacy and mathematics during the Reception year was positively associated with English not the first language. Special needs status, spring/summer term of entry and eligibility for free school meals were all negatively associated with progress.

There was no evidence for any year, for either literacy or maths, that additional staff or additional adults in the class had an effect on children's progress and they did not interact with class size, indicating that there is no apparent 'compensation' effect of having extra adults in the class.

Of the classroom processes, the number of times children were heard to read, the percentage teaching time and inattentive/hyperactive pupil behaviour were all found to influence attainment. However, none of the gains achieved by pupils in smaller classes could be explained in the statistical analysis by these classroom processes. I return to the relationship between class size and classroom processes, drawing on all the information available, not just from these statistical analyses, in Chapter 9.

In Years 1 and 2, there was some evidence that children in smaller classes made more progress in literacy during Year 1 but otherwise there was not strong evidence of an effect of class size upon progress during Years 1 and 2, for either literacy or mathematics. The results indicated that pupils made less progress when moving to classes of a different size from that experienced in the Reception year. For both years, girls made more progress in literacy, while boys made more progress in maths.

There was evidence that the benefit in literacy gained by small classes in the Reception year were still evident at the end of Year 1, though the effect size was reduced. The benefits were no longer evident clearly in mathematics. The benefits of small classes in the Reception year were not clearly evident by the end of Year 2.

9 Class size, educational progress, and classroom processes

What can we conclude?

We know from many studies a good deal about main factors influencing children's progress in the first few years after entry to school (for example, Tizard et al. 1988). We know that children's skills and knowledge on entry to school are important determinants, and we know that income levels (for example, as indicated by free school meals) and gender are also influential. We also know that home influences and parental input are likely to have an influence, as are more endogenous or within-child factors, such as intelligence and concentration. Over and above these influences the effect of school experiences are bound to be relatively small, and, as part of that, the influence of differences in class size is bound to be even smaller.

Given this, the effect of class size that we find in this study can be seen as impressive. Our analyses have demonstrated a clear effect of class size difference on children's academic attainment over the Reception year, both before and after adjusting for possible confounding factors. The effect is comparable to that reported by the experimental STAR project, as we saw in Chapter 8.

Age/year group of child is important

Our results show how vital it is to take account of the age of the child when considering class size effects. The effects are most obvious in the first year in school – the Reception year. This is consistent with the STAR project (Finn and Achilles 1999). There seem to be clear policy implications that follow from these findings. There is a clear case for reducing class sizes at Reception and KS1, and especially Reception. The government's policy of a maximum class size at 30 is certainly consistent with this recommendation, though our results suggest where resources may be further targeted. There is also support for the view that small classes and class size reduction initiatives are best seen as a policy of prevention but not remediation, in the sense that the evidence supports the use of small classes immediately after entry to school, but there is no evidence we have seen that small classes introduced later in children's school lives are as effective.

Our results offer support for a description of class size effects as a 'start-up phenomenon'. This is a term used by Mosteller (1995) to explain the STAR results. Here the explanation of the class size effect cannot be separated from the age of the children; specifically, small classes work because the children are new to school, and because small classes give the child and the teacher the opportunity for children to learn to learn, to learn how to be students.

Benefits for how long?

The effects of class size in the Reception year are still evident on literacy progress at the end of the second year of school (Year 1), though by the end of the third year the effects are not clear. There were no clear longer-term effects of class size differences on mathematics achievement. In one sense this indicates that the early benefits of smaller classes on literacy achievement 'wash out' after two years in school, though it needs to be remembered that the children in this study (in contrast with the STAR project) were not restricted in terms of which size of class they moved to from year to year. A child in a small class could therefore move to a larger class and vice versa. In such circumstances it would be unrealistic to expect a large carry over from year to year, and the continued effect one year after transition into Year 1 is therefore noteworthy. The STAR project indicates that consistency in small class sizes would be needed for continued effects on children's achievements.

The statistical analyses reported in Chapter 8 may underestimate the effects of class size differences in that they are about the effects only on academic achievement scores in literacy and maths. We have seen in other chapters in this book that class size is related to other features of schooling, such as classroom processes like teaching, and these extend beyond the Reception year. There may also be relationships between class size and other features of learning and development not measured in this study.

There may also be longer term effects of class size differences, beyond that evident from study of the first three years of school, and in current research we are following the same children over the next stage of their schooling, i.e., from 7–11 years (KS2) and documenting both class sizes and educational achievement.

'Disruption' effect

In this study we were able to capture the 'real world' of class sizes as they occurred in schools, and so we were able to analyse more precisely the influence of changes in class size from year to year. In our analyses we were able to look at the effect on children's educational progress of changes in class sizes between the Reception year and Year 1. As I showed in Chapter 8, these results revealed what might be called a 'disruption' effect when moving into a different sized class from Reception to Year 1, and this effect was magnified when children moved into a bigger class. The policy implication of this result seems to be that, in addition to smaller classes in the Reception year, it is advisable to maintain stability into future years.

Who benefits?

The results showed that the effect of class size differences varied in some important respects for different kinds of children in the schools. In particular there were differential effects on literacy progress over the reception year for the three attainment groups on entry to school. While all three groups benefited from decreases in class size down to about 25 children, class sizes smaller than this benefited only the lowest attaining group in literacy. This means that decreases in class sizes below 25 continue to have a positive effect on literacy progress for the initially lowest attaining group, but less so for the middle and high attaining groups. For the lowest attaining group of children a reduction in class size from 25 to 15 was associated with a large gain in literacy progress. For mathematics the pattern is somewhat different with all three initial attainment groups benefiting equally from class size reductions.

We believe there are important policy implications arising from these results. As we have seen in general the results support the use of small classes during the first, Reception year. However, the results also allow a more specific picture in terms of the children who most benefit. Small classes appear to work best in literacy for children who are most in need academically, and who thus have most ground to make up. These findings further suggest where targeting of resources (in this case small classes) might be best directed.

An optimum class size?

Is there a 'best' class size? Is small always better? And large always worse? What can we conclude from our research? We have seen that much of the debate in the UK has been about the adverse effects of large classes over 30, and that in the UK there is now a commitment to maximum class sizes of 30 at the Foundation Stage and Key Stage 1. In the USA, the STAR project (Finn and Achilles 1999) and research reviews (for example Slavin 1990) indicate that class size reductions below 20 are necessary before sizeable effects on student performance are seen.

One advantage of our research, in contrast to class size reduction experiments, like the STAR project, is that we did not restrict class sizes, and we can therefore make judgements about the effects of the full range of class sizes found in our schools. Our results suggest a complex picture when it comes to judgements about optimum class sizes. In maths, there are benefits resulting from decreases in class size across the full range of class sizes, not just below 20 in a class. However, in the case of literacy, the size of class below which benefits are most marked, varies according to the child's level of attainment prior to school entry. For the lowest attainers there is a tendency for class size reductions to be most marked when they are 25 and smaller. There are other indications in our study that 25 may be an important number of children, below which relationships with classroom processes, such as the number and size of within-class groups, become most evident (Blatchford et al. 2001a). In our current follow-up research in which we are asking head teachers of children aged 7–11 years about their preferred class size, the most popular answer is 25.

One intriguing possibility is suggested (but not proven) by our results. Although it may be the case that increases in student numbers are likely to be associated with difficulties for teachers and negative effects on children's educational experiences in class, the converse does not necessarily apply. In other words, although there is a tendency to think of all reductions in class size as a good thing, with approximations to one-to-one tutoring the ideal, it may also be worth considering the possibility that class sizes can become *too small*. Interestingly, this was first suggested to us by teachers in our study, who could sometimes find that with too few children in the class the dynamics of the group could become flat, and some children could dominate. This possibility of a threshold *below which* numbers become educationally less positive (rather than the usual concern with a threshold above which numbers become less positive) requires further exploration and testing.

In general it is probably oversimplistic to talk about optimal class sizes in an exact way. Teachers' judgements about preferred class sizes are likely to be affected by what they have experienced and what they perceive as realistically achievable. Judgements are also likely to be affected by culturally bound views about teaching and about learning, and for these reasons it would not be surprising if views differed between countries. For teachers in some countries class sizes of fewer than 20 would be virtually unimaginable! We need, therefore, to be careful about comparisons across countries and attempts to pin down an optimal class size. Having said this, our results suggest that overall decreases of any number (at least in the Reception year) are to be welcomed.

Effects modified by characteristics of children, classes or teachers?

We analysed whether class size effects varied according to characteristics of pupils (such as term of entry, eligibility for free school meals), class characteristics (such as the percentage of children in the class eligible for free school meals, the percentage of children in the class with behaviour difficulties) and teacher characteristics (such as teacher experience and professional training and qualifications). Some of these influenced children's progress (see Chapter 8 for full details), but only one variable appeared to influence the effect of class size on progress over the Reception year. This was the children's term of entry into school. Pupils entering school in the spring or summer term performed less well at the end of the Reception year compared to those entering school in the autumn term. These later entrants were generally found in slightly larger classes than the autumn entrants. This effect is not just a reflection of later entrants being younger, because age of child was also entered into the statistical models. The policy implication of this finding is that staggered entry into school does not on average favour academically the later entrants to school, and this is not just to do with their age. To turn this the other way round, in terms of academic progress there appear to be benefits to children of being in the Reception year for the whole year.

Alternatives to class size reductions

Class size and extra staff and adults

The effect of additional staff and additional adults on pupils' educational progress in maths and literacy was also examined. There was no clear evidence for any year, for either literacy or maths, that additional staff or additional adults in the class had an effect on children's progress, and there was no apparent 'compensation' effect of having extra adults in the class.

This result is consistent with the STAR project, where it was found that there was no compensatory effect of having extra staff in larger (regular) classes. It is also supported by other research (Muijs and Reynolds 2002). The consistency of results from these studies makes depressing reading.

However, we were able to go beyond statistical relationships between the presence of extra staff and students' achievement and look more closely and in a more rounded way at the contribution of teaching assistants. I showed in Chapter 7 that teachers were largely positive about the contribution of teaching assistants but that the case studies revealed considerable variation in their effectiveness, and it was this that was likely to account for the lack of clear associations with children's attainments.

I return to the policy implications of these findings on support staff in schools later in this chapter.

Other alternative staffing arrangements

There is a connected but broader issue concerning alternative ways of deploying teachers to classrooms and students. In some countries and in some schools the deployment of staff to children may be considered to be more salient than the numbers of children in a classroom. In some schools, classroom space may not allow the creation of another classroom, even when there are funds to employ another teacher. It may, therefore, be necessary to think of the best use of teaching staff within the context of existing class sizes. Teachers might be employed in various co-teaching arrangements, for example as 'floating' teachers rotating between larger classes, or working with a subset of particular children, perhaps taking them out from the normal classroom context for particular subjects. It was not part of the original research design to examine these and there is not space in this book to consider them now. It is worth noting, with Wang and Finn (2000), that there is actually little information available that compares, in a systematic way, these alternative models with each other and with class size reduction. This is another area in need of attention.

But is there something special about small classes?

It is therefore sensible to consider carefully alternatives to class size reductions, and ways in which staff are deployed. However, it may also be that there is something intrinsically important about small classes as the basis of an effective educational environment. Small classes may be important because the smaller the group the more intense the engagement of all participants. It should be borne in mind that classroom life is a social and in a sense a theatrical experience, as well as an educational one. The reason that class size is more importantly related to educational achievement than the ratio of pupils to teachers may be that it is not the numbers of pupils to teachers that is crucial but the feature of *smallness* and the opportunity for the development of *a sense of community* which cannot be realized in a larger class (Wang and Finn 2000). In other words, the issue of class size is connected to teachers' and pupils' experience of, and the dynamics of, social contexts, and is not just a matter of numbers of children to adults. This is likely to be particularly the case in a primary classroom where children can spend a good part of their day with one teacher. The pedagogical processes and social dynamics in a small class may be distinctive, and I return to this possibility later.

Classroom processes connected to class size differences

In this book I have examined relations between class size and classroom processes. A feature of the results reported in this book is that they have drawn on multiple methods of data collection, including time allocation estimates, systematic observation, teachers' end of year accounts and case studies, and are based on quantitative and qualitative analyses. Here I summarize the main results under three main headings:

- within-class groups
- effects on teachers
- effects on children.

Within-class groups

In Chapter 3, I showed that class size was related to the size and number of groupings within the classroom. For much of their time in UK primary schools children are seated and work in groups. Teachers' everyday experience was that with a large class there is often a difficult choice between larger or more numerous groups, and that larger groups, at least with children of this age, could have an adverse effect on the amount and quality of teaching and the quality of pupils' work and concentration in these groups. In large classes there are more large groups which present teachers with more difficulties and children with less individual attention. Some teachers felt that it was group size rather than class size which more directly affected their teaching and classroom management. So while debate and research on class size differences has often been in terms of direct effects on attainments, it is important educationally to consider the mediating role of within-class groupings.

Effects on teachers

We found consistent relationships between class size and teaching. In Chapter 4 I drew on quantitative analyses of time allocation estimates and systematic observation, along with qualitative analyses of teachers' end of year accounts and case studies. The results from the two more obviously quantitative components showed that children in small classes were more likely to interact with their teachers, there was more teaching on a one-to-one basis, more times when children were the focus of a teacher's attention, and more teaching overall. In short, there was more teacher task time with pupils. The qualitative data indicated that in smaller classes there was more teacher support for learning, as reflected in the amount of individual attention paid to students, and in terms of the immediate, responsive, sustained and purposeful nature of teacher interactions with children, the depth of a teacher's knowledge about children, and sensitivity to individual children's needs.

Results presented in Chapter 3, though focused on within-class groups, reinforced and supported this account of ways that class size and teaching are related. It was suggested that larger groups (more likely in larger classes) affected the quantity and quality of teaching in terms of the attention that teachers could give each child and groups, the quality and effectiveness of their teaching, the thoroughness of their questioning, the amount of extended adult-intensive tasks, and the depth of their knowledge about individual children. Some of the clearest findings were those in Chapter 5 concerning connections between class size and individual support for reading, in the form of hearing individual children read – a strategy that has been central in the teaching of reading to young children. The quantitative results showed that in large classes children are heard read by their teachers less often and for less time. Qualitative analyses of teachers' questionnaires and case studies indicated important qualitative dimensions that could be affected in large classes. These included the quality of instruction, extending children's reading, and meeting different individual needs, most obviously of less able children, but also more able and children in between these two extremes. The case studies also indicated that pressures of time in larger classes could mean more interruptions and attention to individuals was more superficial.

Results presented in Chapters 3 and 4, particularly those based on teachers' reports and case studies, also indicated that in larger classes teachers spent more time on non-teaching activities and faced more difficulties with classroom management and control.

The results therefore indicate that class size is related to teaching in three main ways:

- teacher task time with pupils
- teacher/individual support for learning
- classroom management and control.

Overall it is proposed that there is support for the notion that in smaller classes there is more likelihood of what we call *teacher support for learning* – more individualization of teaching if you like, though this does not imply that it has to be on a one-to-one basis – it could be in group or whole class contexts.

Our results suggest that while small classes will not make a bad teacher better, they can allow teachers to be more effective; conversely large classes inevitably present teachers with difficulties and the need for compromises. Our results are consistent with other recent comments on relations between class size and teaching, and indicate that small classes can offer *opportunities* for teachers to teach better (Anderson 2000) or, to use a different term, they can create *facilitating conditions* for teachers to teach and students to learn (Wang and Finn 2000).

As explained in Chapter 4, there is a strong suggestion that in a small class a teacher will more easily be able to provide effective 'scaffolding' for the pupils, and this is most important in the early years of schooling, when it needs to be at its most active and sustained. It is interesting that researchers interested in the notion of scaffolding are generally pessimistic about classroom learning. Underlying work in this tradition (for example Tharp and Gallimore 1991; Bliss et al. 1996; Wood and Wood 1996), just as in earlier research by Tizard and Hughes (1984) and Wells (1986), is the advantage of the learning context of informal, usually one-to-one, interactions with an adult in homes, over those found in classrooms. Teachers' interactions with their pupils can be ineffective, sometimes because teacher questioning tends to silence rather than encourage them. The rather provocative conclusion is that schools have much to learn from informal teaching by parents. From this point of view, therefore, school classrooms seem inherently disadvantaged because teachers cannot provide the individualization of scaffolding needed by all children. The problem is likely to be magnified with a large number of children.

It is my view, however, there are limits to the applicability of such approaches, at least as currently expressed, when considering everyday classroom learning. They may not be relevant in the context of situations involving more than one learner. A close reading of our case studies reveals a picture of teaching in classrooms which has distinctive qualities, different to one-to-one tutoring, which will need to be conceptualized in different terms. Some show interactions between teachers and children (usually in small classes) which were judged to be impressive and effective. As said above, there may be something distinctive about the dynamics in a small class that can promote effective instruction and learning. There are also learning processes involved in contacts between children as well as between teachers and children that I consider more fully below. This suggests that classroom learning involving a number of children does not have to be at best a watered-down version of the ideal, that is one-to-one tutoring, and makes the point that we need a *different* view of effective learning in school contexts, and a social pedagogy of classrooms which takes account of the realities of classroom environments, including different numbers of children.

Teacher quality

In Chapter 1, I showed that some have argued that it is not class size that is important but the quality of teaching. Given the prevalence of this view a comment is in order.

The evidence from the California Class Size Reduction Program is that teacher quality was vital. It is now recognized that the haste in finding teachers to implement class size reductions meant that inexperienced teachers were hired and this made the initiative less effective than it should have been. However, the situation in our study was quite different. Our study involved a fairly random selection of schools and teachers, not a recently enlisted group employed for a particular educational initiative. We could not make teachers take part in the study, of course, but this applied to all the teachers in the study. Teachers will obviously vary in a number of ways, including how effective they are in terms of their pupils' progress and classroom control, but we have no reason to believe these prior differences are related to differences in class sizes. Associations between class size and achievement are, in this sense, independent of qualities of the teachers involved.

It might be noted that we did seek to find out whether certain teacher characteristics were associated with class size differences and whether they, rather than class size differences, influenced how well children did in school. One possibility, for example, is that the more experienced or qualified teachers are given the largest and potentially most difficult classes. However (as reported in Chapter 8), we found no evidence that any of the teacher characteristics, such as age, experience, qualifications or training, or the head teacher's rating of their effectiveness, was related to class size or had an influence on progress over any of the three years.

It is true that these characteristics, entered into quantitative analysis, were relatively general and did not capture all essential aspects of effectiveness in teaching. This raises a number of difficult questions about what is meant by teacher quality and effectiveness that it was not possible to address fully in this study. Our general position, however, is that there is a danger in assuming an indefinable quality, in relation to teaching, that cannot be analysed or broken down. In other words, 'quality' of teaching, and aspects of teaching connected to class size differences, must be evident in some way in what teachers *do* in classrooms. We recognized that it would be difficult to cover all the features and qualities that might be seen as manifesting effective teaching, and in this study we tried to capture some important dimensions, identified in previous research as likely to be significant in pupils' educational progress, and then studied to what extent they were related to class size differences and accounted for the effect of class size differences on pupils' educational progress. In other words, teacher quality is not something separate from the features of teaching we have examined in relation to class size differences. This is not meant to imply that teachers will not vary in the success with which they adapt to different class sizes, and I come back to this shortly.

Effects on children

Results shown in Chapters 3, 4 and 6 when taken together indicate three main ways that class size affects children.

Active involvement with the teacher

The observation results presented in Chapter 4 showed that in smaller classes children not only received more contacts from teachers but also had a more active role themselves in interactions with their teachers, in terms of initiating and responding. This finding was supported by teacher reports and case studies shown in Chapters 3 and 4.

Pupil attentiveness and off-task behaviour

Results from the systematic observation study showed that children in large classes were more likely to be off-task. This was evident in contacts with their teachers – they were less likely to attend to the teacher and to be off-task in contacts with them; in contacts with other children – they were more likely to be actively off-task with other children; and when on their own – they were more likely to be off-task when on their own, especially in the passive form of being disengaged from allocated work. Results from the teacher-completed pupil behaviour ratings (presented in Chapter 6) were less clear, though there were weak but significant relationships between class size and distractibility. These results were supported by qualitative analyses (presented in Chapter 3) which showed that teachers found that in smaller groups (more likely in smaller classes) it was easier for pupils to concentrate.

There is then some confirmation across both quantitative and qualitative results that children in large classes will be more distracted from work and more often off-task. These results offer support for the view of Finn and Achilles (1999) that one of the main effects of class size is on children's attentiveness in class.

Peer relations

Previous research did not allow strong predictions about the likely effect of class size on social relations between children, but results (shown in Chapter 6) did go against our general expectation. Social relations between children as revealed in the PBR were not strongly related to class size, but it was found that there was a slight though consistent tendency for worse peer relations, in terms of aggression and rejection of peers, in the smallest classes. Intriguingly, then, there were signs that relationships between children are *worse* in small classes with fewer than 20 children. Smaller classes may be better academically but not necessarily socially! It needs to be stressed, however, that this finding needs further research and replication.

These results on connections between class size and pupil behaviour need to be seen in the context of our observation results reported in Chapters 4 and 6 which showed that class size differences affect the balance between teacher–pupil and pupil–pupil interactions. Children in larger classes spend more time with each other, interacting about work, socially, and also mucking about, while children in smaller classes interact more with their teachers.

If one starts from the assumption that teacher–child contacts are likely to be the most conducive social context for learning and achievement then the situation in large classes is worrying. However, one should not quickly dismiss the view that task-related contacts between peers are unimportant. Although children engaged in more off-task behaviours overall (mostly attributable to off-task behaviours when with their teachers and when not interacting), at the same time they engaged in more on-task-related behaviours with their peers. This can be seen in positive and negative terms. If children, by being less able to get a teacher's attention, are then forced to turn their attentions to each other then this may be a distracting influence and not productive. On the other hand, using other children as sources of information and collaboration may actually be a valuable context for learning. One interesting result to emerge in Chapter 3 was that in smaller classes there were fewer instances of children in groups working toward a group product – in other words, there was less cooperative/collaborative group work in smaller classes. This indicates that one strategy in larger classes would be for teachers to set up tasks involving peer collaboration as an alternative to the possibly fruitless, and certainly tiring, quest for more teacher individualized attention.

Much will depend on the quality of interactions between peers, which were not examined in the present study. Descriptive research has shown that the level of talk in pupil groups can be low level and unchallenging (Bennett et al. 1994), even though in terms of definitions used in this study they would still have been classified as task related. A number of authors are now recognizing the potential of peer interactive contexts in relation to achievement and motivation (O'Donnell and King 1999); this in turn suggests that one type of strategy teachers could make when faced with larger classes is to make more deliberate use of peer collaboration. This will require helping pupils to work productively together, for example, in terms of gaining trust and confidence in each other, listening to each other, and giving and receiving explanations (Webb and Falivar 1999), as well as attention to group sizes (Kutnick et al. 2002). I shall return to this point shortly.

Two other effects of class size differences

I also briefly note two other factors, suggested by the qualitative analyses of teacher reports and case studies, which were seen as connected to class size differences, but which were less strongly supported by the study. These suggestions are in need of further verification.

Curriculum coverage

The results presented in Chapters 3, 4 and 6 suggest that class size differences can influence the depth of curriculum coverage. In further analyses not reported in this book, we did not find clear connections between class size differences and the amount of time that teachers spent in the main curriculum areas of maths and literacy. This is not surprising, especially now that in the UK there are clear guidelines about time to be spent in literacy and maths. Overall, our results suggest that it is the quality of teaching within curriculum areas that is related to class size differences, not the amount of time spent in coverage.

Quality of children's work

There were suggestions from teacher reports and case studies (as reported in Chapters 3 and 4) concerning difficulties of maintaining and supporting high quality work in larger classes.

Limitations of the study

There are several potential limitations of this study. There may be other classroom processes related to class size differences that were not covered. Any study has to be selective and, although aspects of classroom processes were selected carefully on the basis of previous research and our visits to schools, there are bound to be aspects, perhaps connected to class size differences, that we have not included.

We would be the first to admit that we concentrated rather precisely, and some might argue narrowly, on the academic outcomes of literacy and maths. We did this deliberately, not the least because we believe that they are important indicators. However, it is quite possible that the effects of class size differences may also be found in other aspects of children's work, for example, in terms of more creative and artistic areas, and in terms of other 'outcomes' like problem solving, not easily captured in tests of achievement, and not studied in our research. Indeed, as suggested previously, it may be that with the advent in the UK of literacy and numeracy strategies, and mandated time in each, that it is more likely to be other non-core areas that will suffer in larger classes. Anecdotally we know that teachers feel that time devoted to literacy and numeracy sessions means that there is now less time available for more creative and artistic activities and this might be expected to be especially true in larger classes. However, this possibility awaits further study.

Another potential limitation of the research is the time when it took place. All educational research is historically located and (as has been said) there have been more recent initiatives. I have already commented on changes in legislation in the UK in favour of a maximum class size of 30 at Reception and KS1. Another change has been the rearrangement of the stages of education for young pupils such that the Reception year (the year in school when children become 5 years) is now classified as the last year of the Foundation Stage. This change was in response to (many people's) concerns that the arrangements for KS1 were not appropriate for children who were sometimes just 4 years of age. The change was accompanied by guidance from government organizations on curriculum planning and learning goals for the Foundation Stage. There is not space here to enter into a debate about this change but, whatever the merits or otherwise, the question we do need to address is whether it affects the interpretation of the research findings presented in this book. It is difficult to answer this question with any certainty, not the least because we do not have systematic information on just how much change in reality there has been in the Reception year. The curriculum guidance for the Foundation Stage, offered by government agencies, stresses the need for differentiation to meet the varying needs and stages of development of pupils. This more child-centred approach is likely to mean that, if anything, the number of children in the class will be *even more* important. The connection between class size and teacher support for learning, found in this research, is likely to be even more relevant when the stress is on sensitivity to individual needs and rates of development.

The new structure for early education stresses areas other than literacy and numeracy, such as play, creative development, personal, social and emotional development. I have already commented on the need to study effects on these areas. But these changes do not invalidate the relationships we found between class size and progress in literacy and numeracy during the Reception year. Both areas are still prominent in curriculum guidance for the Foundation Stage and we know from visits to Reception classes at the time of writing how prominent they are in the build up to Y1 and the start of KS1. Furthermore, we know that more and more children are experiencing a full year in the Reception class, and this is likely to make the effects of class size during the Reception year even more widespread.

Affective considerations: compensatory efforts

There is another likely effect of class size differences which also illustrates one of the complexities involved when seeking to establish causal connections with achievement. Effective teaching may be possible in large classes, but this may be at some cost to teachers, for example, in terms of working that much harder, and in terms of eating away at spaces like breaks in the day. It may also affect a teacher's professional satisfaction and enthusiasm. This connection is not, to date, clearly shown in our quantitative results, but we found, particularly in the case studies and end of year questionnaires, that teachers' experiences of class sizes are connected to their emotional involvement in the job of teaching. This was nicely captured by Cahen et al. (1983) in the words of a second grade teacher: 'There's more space; everyone can breathe . . . There's more of ME left at the end of the day!' It was very clear that some teachers in our study with large classes felt that they could not provide the quality of education they felt was important for young children, at least not without a good deal of effort on their part, and this upset them. This gap between a vision of what is appropriate for young children and the realities of teaching a large class may be particularly wide in the case of teachers of the youngest children in school. This theme is taken up more fully in Moriarty et al. (2001).

This suggests that there may be a 'compensation effect', which may serve to cushion the expected effects of larger classes. Expected relations between class size and pupil outcomes may therefore be minimized because of teachers' level of commitment, driven by their professional self-perception. If this is true then relations between class size and outcomes are complicated by ways in which teachers may *compensate* for the expected negative effects – a nice example of how a simple model of causality does not work in real life! This also indicates that efforts to capture teacher quality, as just discussed, or to control for the possibly non-random allocation of classes to teachers (for example, the possibility that the more experienced teachers are given the larger and or more difficult classes), when examining relations between class size and outcomes, may still miss the possibility that teachers adapt in dynamic ways to the conditions under which they find themselves in classrooms, and this will include the number of children in the class.

A summary model of the effect of class size differences on classroom processes and outcomes

A general point about the effects of class size differences on classroom processes can now be made. As I have said, there has been increasing recognition that we need accounts of classroom behaviour that might explain why smaller classes might affect academic outcomes. In the Institute of Education class size study we have gone some distance in identifying ways that teachers and pupils are affected by size of class. Our research suggests that it is not likely, or realistic, to think that one theory or conceptual framework will account for effects. Class size effects are, in other words, *not singular but multiple*. Accordingly, we shall need multiple theoretical or conceptual frameworks to account for these effects and to judge their implications, such as those connected to teaching, pupil attentiveness and social relations. Further, the different effects may have conflicting outcomes, for example in the sense that smaller classes can lead to positive academic outcomes but problematic social effects. Picking up on the point just made about teachers' compensatory efforts suggests a further complication, in that not only may there be multiple effects but also different effects can themselves affect each other, so that, for example, teachers may make extra efforts to hear children read because they know that a larger class has limited the time available for this activity during lesson time.

It would be difficult to capture all the possible complexities involved, but as a way of summarizing and integrating the main classroom processes reported in this book, that are related to class size differences, I have prepared Figure 9.1. In doing so I have taken up Anderson's (2000) challenge, when he called for revisions and updating of his own model. The model draws together results from both qualitative and qualitative analyses.

Figure 9.1 is designed to be a descriptive summary of findings rather than exact portrayal of statistical relationships or causal paths. Some connections are likely to be stronger than others, for example, because they are suggested by both quantitative and qualitative analyses. In line with Anderson's (2000) introduction to his own model, this is not meant to be the 'right 'model but rather a best description of relationships suggested in our study.

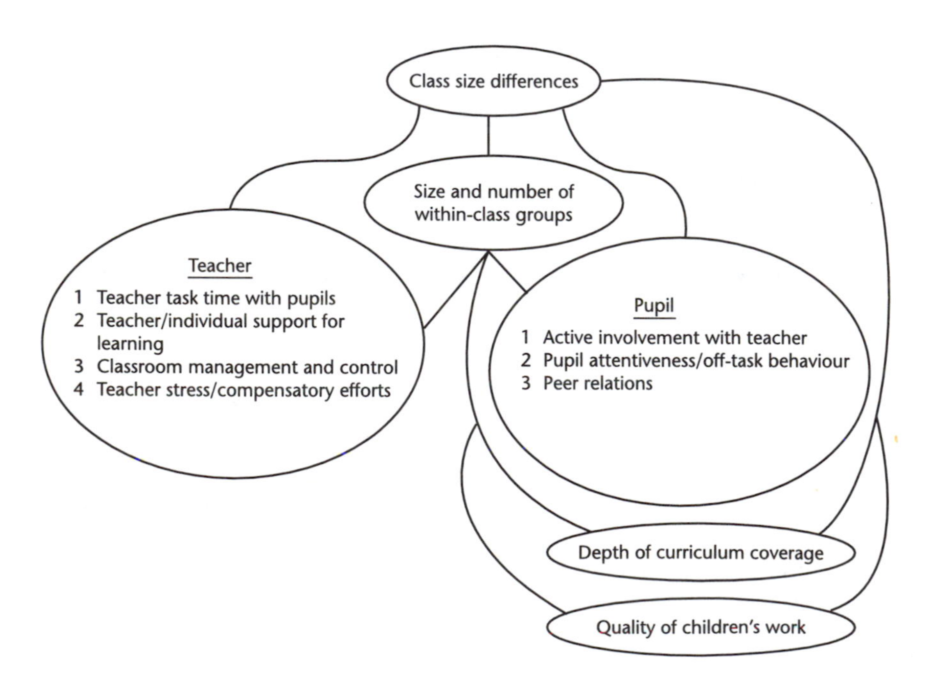

Figure 9.1 Connections between class size and classroom processes

The first thing to note is that the model adds in one important component, extra to Anderson's model. It shows that class size is related to within-class grouping practices such as the size and number of groups. And as we have seen, these are related to several classroom processes. I have indicated, with lines, connections between features in the figure.

Figure 9.1, then, shows that class size is related to four processes connected to the teacher. These have already been summarized in this chapter. They are teacher task time with pupils, teacher/individual support for learning, classroom management and control, and teacher stress/ compensatory effects.

A separate bubble shows that class size is also likely to be related to pupil aspects. These are listed under three headings given earlier in this chapter: active involvement with the teacher, pupil attentiveness and off-task behaviour, and peer relations. One problematic area is also highlighted. There is likely to be more child–child interaction in larger classes and some evidence that peer relations are less good in smaller classes, but this needs further testing.

I have also added the depth of curriculum coverage and the quality of student work though again these are suggested rather than proven.

The role of mediating variables

In this study we have found, and Figure 9.1 shows, that class size is related to pupil progress over the Reception year, and that class size is related to several classroom processes. (In the interests of clarity, I have not attempted in Figure 9.1 to show links between classroom processes and student achievement.) But as we saw in Chapter 8, there was little evidence from the full statistical analysis that the classroom processes had a mediating role in the relation between class size and achievement. To take an example, although class size is related to teaching time and (not shown) teaching time is related to progress, it is not possible to say on the basis of our statistical results (see Chapter 8) that teaching time mediates the effect of class size differences on attainment. This is in a sense a disappointing result though methodological features of our study might have underestimated some effects. Some of the 'process' measures, such as on teaching time, were relatively broad and measured not at the child but the more general class level. They are therefore less sensitive than measures at the individual child. As mentioned above our main statistical analysis was also limited to general measures of academic outcome. There is the possibility that dimensions studied may therefore be, on conceptual grounds, the right aspects but may not have been measured with sufficient strength and sensitivity.

There is also the point that any kind of statistical analysis, no matter how sophisticated, rests on quantification, and it may be that some essential processes and their effects cannot be captured in this way. We have discussed this possibility elsewhere (Blatchford et al. 1998). It may be that a smaller class size allows a teacher to approach children in a more personalized and more humanistic way, but this would be hard to measure and then enter into statistical analysis!

Having said this, the statistical analyses have been helpful in narrowing down the likely processes connected to class size and to progress, and this study has, therefore, helped identify the variables that could be fruitfully examined in future research. The more qualitative analyses have also indicated aspects possibly linked with class size that could be followed up. There are, therefore, a number of leads from this study concerning where future research should be best targeted, in particular the aspects of teacher and pupil behaviour listed in Figure 9.1.

Class size as a classroom contextual variable

The results presented in this book raise questions about traditional ways of viewing the effects of teaching and instruction. As I argued in Chapter 1, these have tended to be viewed in terms of a direct model, where teachers' actions toward pupils are seen as having effects on pupils' learning or attainments. Our study, however, supports a contextual approach, within which class size differences have effects on both teachers and pupils.

As I showed in Chapter 1, it has been argued by both researchers and politicians that it is not size of class that is the problem, or the solution, but the quality of teaching and teacher training. This argument is, of course, convenient for policy makers because responsibility is then attached to the teacher. But in terms of the classroom contextual influences described here, this argument is far too simple. Our results suggest that it is not just down to the teacher. In contrast to a direct model, it is not entirely the teacher's responsibility; contextual factors cannot be ignored. Teachers will vary in their effectiveness, but the size of the class and the size of the groups in the class necessarily affect what a teacher has to deal with, and can present her with choices and the need for compromises. Class size is therefore one environmental contextual factor that will influence teachers and pupils in a number of ways. It is not, as Rivkin et al. (2000) imply a case of either supporting teacher training to improve teacher quality, or reducing class sizes. We need to consider both together, and ways of making the most of the opportunities of smaller classes.

Dealing with class size differences: implications for teaching

So bearing this contextual approach in mind, let us return to the nature of the relationship between class size and classroom processes, particularly teaching and peer relations. We have seen that a small class has the potential to allow teachers to provide more extensive and task-related individualization of instruction. So an important next step in this analysis concerns how the teacher *deals* with this classroom contextual feature, that is, with class size. The teacher can deal with it inappropriately. Evertson and Randolph (1989) have offered a fascinating account of observations in STAR small classes. They argue that the adherence of teachers to established methods of reading and maths instruction (as well as the mandated curriculum in Tennessee, which emphasizes basic skills) may have minimized differences between processes in small and regular classes. They describe a teacher in a small class – of fewer than 20 – teaching to one group of 10 while the other children got on with individual work, and then later switching to the other group to teach exactly the same material. They felt this unnecessary repetition was down to inflexibility in the assumption that this size of group works best in the teaching of reading. In a similar way, our case studies indicated that some teachers varied in how successfully they adapted to the number of children in the class. For instance, they indicated that one feature of smaller classes – a tendency to allow immediate feedback – could lead to frequent interruptions, and needs to be watched carefully by teachers. It would of course be absurd to argue that small classes lead to more interruptions. Rather, there is a potential for interruptions in a situation where children expect to have their demands met instantly – and this is an expectation they can develop in a small class.

On the other hand a teacher can deal with small classes effectively. We have documented examples of teachers in small classes doing a marvellous job – with observers coming away inspired by the quality of teaching and children's educational experiences. In these classrooms teachers were taking full advantage of the extra opportunities for individual, focused and sustained attention provided by small classes. The benefits of having fewer children will not flow in any natural way – indeed, as we have seen, the benefits resulting from more contact with children can create problems, in terms of interruptions. Teachers have to work just as hard to manage learning effectively. Evertson et al. (1981) showed that teachers skilled in classroom management were able to make adjustments necessary to cope with academically diverse classes, but that less skilled teachers were not.

Implications for teacher training and professional development

There is a good deal of agreement that unless teachers actually change their style of teaching in response to class size differences there will be little benefit from smaller classes. This was recognized long ago by Haberman and Larson (1968): 'If smaller classes are to make a difference in classroom behaviours of teachers, it may be that they need to be instructed on how to teach a small class in different ways.'

Galton et al. (1996) consider how to make the most of the opportunities provided by smaller classes, in terms of opportunities for sustained and responsive contacts. They suggest that there is not likely to be much preparation in initial teacher training concerning ways of adapting teaching to class size. When they get their own class they are left to adapt to it on their own. Galton et al. (1996) suggest allowing student teachers opportunities with smaller classes, for example with half the class, while the teacher takes the other half in another location. This would help the student teacher gain experience of teaching the whole class, and getting experience of the kind of sustained and focused teaching that Maurice Galton and many others recommend.

My view is that there should be a place in teacher training and professional development work for a close consideration of classroom contextual features, of which the number of children in the class is one. This is not just a matter of 'instructing' would-be and practising teachers – this is too simplistic a model. Rather, it is flexibility in the face of changing classroom contexts that seems important. Our results suggest that this should be directed at maximizing the opportunities for individualized support and also making productive use of other contexts for learning, particularly group work.

The issue of training and preparation also applies to support staff in schools. This is a matter of huge importance world-wide. Finn et al. (2000) point out, with regard to the situation in the USA, that teacher education programmes often lack any preparation for supervising or negotiating responsibilities with a teaching assistant, and popular texts used in teacher training courses do not address the presence of an assistant in the classroom. Finn et al. (2000) conclude that urgent action needs to be taken. They argue that

> the greatest payoff [is to] remedy the deficient preparation of paraprofessionals for the tasks they perform, the lack of clearly defined roles for aides in the classroom, and the absence of training for teachers in utilizing their assistants. That these functions are largely ignored today is all too apparent.
>
> (Finn et al. 2000: 165)

They also point out that paraprofessionals in other fields like law or medicine undertake extensive training for their roles, have well-defined responsibilities in what they do, and clear career paths.

In the UK there are increasing numbers of such staff in classrooms and it is vital not only that we plan carefully their training and professional development, but also that we consider their role and deployment in teachers' professional training and development.

I am pleased that in the UK this problem has been recognized and acted on by the government and is reflected in the initiative to improve the training and provision of teaching assistants. Our study shows several ways in which the initiative could be specifically targeted. It was concluded, especially on the basis of the case studies, that the pedagogical role of teaching assistants should not be overlooked. We are not sure that this is dealt with as fully as it could be in training materials we have seen. As I showed in Chapter 7, the simple fact is that TAs *will* to a greater or less degree be involved in teaching; in other words they will be involved in face-to-face interactions with pupils that have an educational or pedagogical purpose. So, as well as considering ways in which they can support literacy and numeracy strategies, which is clearly important, we also have to consider ways that TAs can engage to good effect in all everyday teaching interactions with children. In Chapter 7 I showed that this raises questions about the distinctive contributions of TAs and teachers. Can the contribution of TAs in this aspect at least be considered in the same terms as the teacher's? If not, what is different? This is a controversial area with teacher associations understandably concerned that paraprofessionals should be expected to do the same job as the teachers they represent, who have higher qualifications and more extensive training. But this is an issue that cannot be avoided.

So overall there is a need in the design of teacher training programmes, both initial and continuing, to consider ways of adjusting productively to contextual features like class size. It is not, as some imply, a case of either supporting teacher training to improve teacher quality, or reducing class sizes. We need to consider both together, and ways of making the most of the opportunities of smaller classes and ways of dealing with large classes. There is an allied need to plan for the effective deployment of teaching assistants and other adults in educational settings.

Don't forget other contexts for learning: group work

There is another aspect of the way that teachers can take good advantage of the opportunities afforded by smaller classes. A main theme arising out of our results has been the potential benefits in small classes of the greater likelihood of individual support for learning. But one danger that should be warned against is to see all the benefits of smaller classes in terms of increased opportunities for individualized teaching. We need to be careful not to overlook the benefits that can stem from other contexts for learning. In particular there is no guarantee that smaller classes will automatically lead to more productive work in groups. As we saw in Chapter 3, the benefits of smaller groups in terms of teacher attention and the quality of pupil work did not extend to more cooperative group work. There was if anything less cooperative group work in smaller classes. Teachers did not seem to recognize the possible benefits of smaller classes for more productive group work.

There may be particular implications here for teachers in larger classes. As we saw in Chapters 4 and 6, pupils are likely to interact more with each other in larger classes, and one way teachers might make the most of large classes is to consider helping the children toward effective group work. However, in research I have conducted with Peter Kutnick we have found that, despite the potential for group work as a valuable context for learning, and despite the fact that students *will* be involved in group work anyway, there was in reality very little high quality group work and teachers and pupils were not prepared for it. Overall we found that teachers had little faith in student's ability to work in groups, and groups were not set up or prepared with a clear educational purpose. Students themselves were worried about working in groups (Blatchford et al. 2001c).

It is important therefore to consider smaller units than the whole class. This was recognized in the 1980s by Cahen et al. (1983: 207) who argued: 'Instead of class size, perhaps we should investigate grouping arrangements and alternatives for organization at the school and classroom level which provide small-class conditions for some children and/or for part of the school day.' But we would go further. We argue that groups within the class should be considered not just in terms of increasing teacher attention to pupils, but in terms of taking seriously relatively pupil self-directed group work in classes. A teacher need not be a 'sage on the stage' at all times. Even in small classes the teacher can afford to be a 'guide on the side'!

Summary

The main results and policy implications arising from our research can be summed up as follows:

- There is a clear effect of class size differences on children's academic attainment over the Reception year, and there is a clear case for small class sizes during the first year of school for both literacy and maths.
- Small classes (below 25) work best in literacy for children who are most in need academically, that is, those with the lowest school entry

scores who have most ground to make up. These findings suggest where targeting of resources (in this case small classes) might be best directed.

- There is what might be called a 'disruption' effect when moving into a different sized class from Reception to Year 1. This effect was magnified when children moved into a bigger class. The implication seems to be that in addition to smaller classes in the Reception year it is advisable to maintain stability into future years.
- Pupils entering school not at the beginning of the school year but later, in the spring or summer term, performed less well than those entering school in the autumn term. The policy implication of this finding is that staggered entry into school does not favour academically the later, usually spring term, entrants to school. This is not just to do with their age. To turn this the other way round, in terms of academic progress there appear to be benefits to children of being in the Reception year for the whole year.
- There was no clear evidence for any year for either literacy or maths that additional staff or additional adults in the class had an effect on children's progress in literacy and mathematics and there is no apparent 'compensation' effect of having extra adults in the class.

Class size was related to three main types of classroom processes.

- *Within-class groups:* in larger classes there were larger and more numerous within-class groupings. Teachers found with a large class there was often a difficult choice between larger or more numerous groups, and that larger groups could have an adverse effect on the amount and quality of teaching and the quality of pupils' work and concentration.
- *Class size and teaching:* we found that class size is related to teaching in three main ways: teacher task time with pupils, teacher support for learning, and classroom management and control. Overall it is proposed that in smaller classes there is more likelihood of what we call *teacher support for learning*.
- *Class size and pupils:* we found that in smaller classes there is more active involvement with teacher, in terms of initiating and responding, there was less pupil inattentiveness and off-task behaviour, especially in terms of being disengaged from allocated work, and children in larger classes spent more time interacting with peers. Social relations between children were not strongly related to class size, but intriguingly, there were signs that relationships between children are *worse* in small classes with fewer than 20 children.

Theoretically, class size can be considered as one type of classroom environmental contextual factor that will influence teachers and pupils in a number of ways. In contrast to a direct model of educational influence, we argue that it is not entirely the teacher's responsibility, and contextual factors cannot be ignored.

Finally, there is a need in the design of teacher training programmes, both initial and continuing, to consider ways of adjusting productively to contextual features like class size, and an allied need to plan for the effective deployment of teaching assistants and other adults in educational settings.

References

Achilles, C.M. (1999) *Let's Put Kids First, Finally*. Thousand Oaks, CA: Corwin Press.

Achilles, C.M. and Finn, J.D. (2000) Should class size be the cornerstone for educational policy?, in M.C. Wang and J.D. Finn (eds) *How Small Classes Help Teachers Do their Best*. Philadelphia, PA: Temple University Center for Research in Human Development.

Alexander, R., Rose, J. and Woodhead, C. (1992) *Curriculum Organization and Classroom Practice in Primary Schools: A Discussion Paper*. London: Department of Education and Science.

Anderson, L.W. (2000) Why should reduced class size lead to increased student achievement?, in M.C. Wang and J.D. Finn (eds) *How Small Classes Help Teachers Do their Best*. Philadelphia, PA: Temple University Center for Research in Human Development.

Arends, R.I. (1994) *Learning to Teach*, 3rd edn. New York: McGraw-Hill.

Avon Reception Entry Assessment (1996) Avon Education Department and the Institute of Education.

Barker, R. (1968) *Ecological Psychology*. Stanford, CA: Stanford University Press.

Bassey, M. (1996) Inspection, unlike research, is disinterested!, *Research Intelligence*, 55: 30–2.

Bennett, N. (1996) Class size in primary schools: perceptions of head teachers, chairs of governors, teachers and parents, *British Educational Research Journal*, 22(1): 33–55.

Bennett, N. and Dunne, E. (1992) *Managing Groups*. Hemel Hempstead: Simon and Schuster Education.

Bennett, N., Desforges, C., Cockburn, A. and Wilkinson, B. (1994) *The Quality of Pupil Learning Experiences*. London: Erlbaum.

Betts, J.R. and Shkolnik, J.L. (1999) The behavioural effects of variations in class size: the case of math teachers, *Educational Evaluation and Policy Analysis*, 21(20): 193–213.

Blatchford, P. (in press) A systematic observational study of teachers' and pupils' behaviour in large and small classes, *Learning and Instruction*.

Blatchford, P. and Martin, C. (1998) The effects of class size on classroom processes: 'It's a bit like a treadmill – working hard and getting nowhere fast!', *British Journal of Educational Studies*, 46(2): 118–37.

Blatchford, P. and Mortimore, P. (1994) The issue of class size for young children in schools: what can we learn from research?, *Oxford Review of Education*, 20(4): 411–28.

Blatchford, P., Battle, S. and Mays, J. (1982) *The First Transition: Home to Pre-school.* Windsor: NFER-Nelson.

Blatchford, P., Burke, J., Farquhar, C., Plewis, I. and Tizard, B. (1987) A systematic observation study of children's behaviour at infant school, *Research Papers in Education*, 2(1): 47–62.

Blatchford, P., Goldstein, H. and Mortimore, P. (1998) Research on class size effects: a critique of methods and a way forward, *International Journal of Educational Research*, 29: 691–710.

Blatchford, P., Kutnick, P. and Baines, E. (1999) *The Nature and Use of Classroom Groups in Primary Schools*. Final report to ESRC.

Blatchford, P., Baines, E., Kutnick, P. and Martin, C. (2001a) Classroom contexts: connections between class size and within class grouping, *British Journal of Educational Psychology*, 71(2): 283–302.

Blatchford, P., Baines, E. and Pellegrini, A. (2001b) *A Typology of Playground Involvement: Individual Differences and their Correlates*. Part of symposium on: Playground games and social relations: their social context in elementary/primary school presented at biennial conference of the Society for Research in Child Development, April, Minneapolis.

Blatchford, P., Kutnick, P., Clark, H., McIntyre, H. and Baines, E. (2001c) *The Nature and Use of Within Class Groupings in Secondary Schools*. Final report to ESRC.

Blatchford, P., Goldstein, H., Martin, C. and Browne, W. (2002a) A study of class size effects in English school reception year classes, *British Educational Research Journal*, 28(2): 169–85.

Blatchford, P., Martin, C., Moriarty, V., Bassett, P. and Goldstein, H. (2002b) *Pupil Adult Ratio Differences and Educational Progress over Reception and Key Stage 1*, Research report no. 335. London: Department for Education and Skills.

Blatchford, P., Moriarty, V., Edmonds, S. and Martin, C. (2002c) Relationships between class size and teaching: a multi-method analysis of English infant schools, *American Educational Research Journal*, 39(1): 101–32.

Blatchford, P., Bassett, P., Goldstein, H. and Martin, C. (in preparation) Is small better? Class size, academic progress and classroom processes in children aged 4–7 years.

Bliss, J., Askew, M. and Macrae, S. (1996) Effective teaching and learning: scaffolding revisited, *Oxford Review of Education*, 22(1): 37–61.

Bohrnstedt, G.W., Stecher, BM. and Wiley, E.W. (2000) The California Class Size Reduction Evaluation: lessons learned, in M.C. Wang and J.D. Finn (eds) *How Small Classes Help Teachers Do Their Best*. Philadelphia, PA: Temple University Center for Research in Human Development and Education.

Bronfenbrenner, U. (1979) *The Ecology of Human Development*. Cambridge, MA: Harvard University Press.

Brophy, J. and Good, T. (1986) Naturalistic studies of teacher expectation effects. Reprinted in M. Hammersley (ed.) *Case Studies in Classroom Research*. Milton Keynes: Open University Press.

Cahen, L.S., Filby, N., McCutcheon, G. and Kyle, D.W. (1983) *Class Size and Instruction*. New York and London: Longman.

Cleave, S., Jowett, S. and Bate, M. (1982) . . . *And So to School: A Study of Continuity from Pre-School to Infant School*. Windsor: NFER-Nelson.

Coie, J.D. and Dodge, K.A. (1998) Aggression and antisocial behaviour, in W. Damon (ed.) and N. Eisenberg (vol. ed.) *Handbook of Child Psychology: Volume 3: Social Emotional and Personality Development*. New York: John Wiley.

Cooper, H.M. (1989) Does reducing student-to-teacher ratios affect achievement?, *Educational Psychologist*, 24(1): 79–98.

Creemers, B. (1994) *The Effective Classroom*. London: Cassell.

Croll, P. (1986) *Systematic Classroom Observation*. London: Falmer.

Day, C., Tolley, H., Hadfield, M., Parking, E. and Watling, R. (1996) *Class Research and the Quality of Education*, Report for National Association of Headteachers. Nottingham: Centre for Teacher Development and School Improvement, School of Education, University of Nottingham.

Delamont, S. and Hamilton, D. (1986) Revisiting classroom research: a continuing cautionary tale, in M. Hammersley (ed.) *Controversies in Classroom Research*. Milton Keynes: Open University Press.

Department for Education and Employment (1998) *Teachers: Meeting the Challenge of Change* (Green Paper). London: The Stationery Office.

Department for Education and Employment (2000) *Working with Teaching Assistants: A Good Practice Guide*. London: The Stationery Office.

Dunkin, M.J. and Biddle, B. (1974) *The Study of Teaching*. New York: Holt, Rinehart and Winston.

Evertson, C.M. and Randolph, C.H. (1989) Teaching practices and class size: a new look at an old issue, *Peabody Journal of Education*, 67(1): 85–105.

Evertson, C.M., Sanford, J.P. and Emer, E.T. (1981) Effects of class heterogeneity in Junior High School, *American Educational Research Journal*, 18(2): 219–32.

Farrell, P., Balshaw, M. and Polat, F. (1999) The management, role and training of LSAs. Paper presented to British Educational Research Association, Brighton, September.

Finn, J.D. and Achilles, C.M. (1999) Tennessee's Class Size Study: findings, implications, misconceptions, *Educational Evaluation and Policy Analysis*, 21(2): 97–109.

Finn, J.D., Gerber, S.B., Farber, S.L. and Achilles, C.M. (2000) Teacher aides: an alternative to small classes?, in M.C. Wang and J.D. Finn (eds) *How Small Classes Help Teachers Do their Best*. Philadelphia, PA: Temple University Center for Research in Human Development.

Galton, M., Simon, B. and Croll, B. (1980) *Inside the Primary Classroom*. London: Routledge and Kegan Paul.

Galton, M., Hargreaves, L. and Pell, A. (1996) *Class Size, Teaching and Pupil Achievement*. Leicester University/National Union of Teachers.

Galton, M., Hargreaves, L., Comber, C., Wall, D. with Pell, A. (1999) *Inside the Primary Classroom: 20 Years On*. London and New York: Routledge.

Glass, G., Cahen, L., Smith, M.L. and Filby, N. (1982) *School Class Size*. Beverly Hills, CA: Sage.

Goldstein, H. (1995) *Multilevel Statistical Models*. London: Edward Arnold.

Goldstein, H. and Blatchford, P. (1998) Class size and educational achievement: a review of methodology with particular reference to study design, *British Educational Research Journal*, 24(3): 255–68.

Grissmer, D. (1999) Class size effects: assessing the evidence, its policy implications, and future research agendas, *Educational Evaluation and Policy Analysis*, 21(2): 231–48.

Haberman, M. and Larson, R.G. (1968) Would cutting class size change instruction?, National Elementary Principal, XLVII (Feb.), 18–19.

Haberman, M. and Larson, R.G. (1968) in D.H. Lindbloom (1970) *Class Size as it Affects Instructional Procedures and Educational Outcomes*. Minneapolis, MN: Educational Research and Development Council for the Twin Cities Metropolitan Area.

Hanushek, E.A. (1999) The evidence on class size, in S. Mayer and P. Peterson (eds) *Earning and Learning: How Schools Matter*. Washington, DC: Brookings Institution Press.

Harder, H. (1990) A critical look at reduced class size, *Contemporary Education*, 62(1): 28–30.

Ireson, J. and Blatchford, P. (1993) *The Teaching of Reading in Primary Schools: Final Report of Research Project*. Report submitted to Esmee Fairbairn Trust, London.

Johnson, D. and Johnson, R. (1987) *Learning Together and Alone*. Englewood Cliffs, NJ: Prentice Hall.

Kounin, J.J. and Gump, P.V. (1974) Signal systems of lesson settings and the task-related pre-school children, *Journal of Educational Psychology*, 66(4), 554–62.

Kutnick, P. (1994) Use and effectiveness of groups in classrooms, in P. Kutnick and C. Rogers (eds) *Groups in Schools*. London: Cassell.

Kutnick, P., Blatchford, P. and Baines, E. (2002) Pupil groupings in primary school classrooms: sites for learning and social pedagogy?, *British Educational Research Journal*, 28(2): 187–206.

Ladd, G.W. and Profilet, S.M. (1996) *Child Behavior Scale*. Urbana, IL: University of Illinois at Urbana-Champaign.

LEA Class Size Research Project (1996) *Avon Reception Entry Assessment*. London: Institute of Education, University of London.

Lee, B. and Mawson, C. (1998) *Survey of Classroom Assistants*. Slough: NFER and UNISON.

Lou, Y., Abrami, P.C., Spence, J.C. et al. (1996) Within-class grouping: a meta-analysis, *Review of Educational Research*, 66(4): 423–58.

McGuire, J. and Richman, N. (1988) *Pre-School Behaviour Checklist (PBCL) Handbook*. Windsor: NFER-Nelson.

McIntyre, D. and Macleod, G. (1986) The characteristics and uses of systematic observation, in M. Hammersley (ed.) *Controversies in Classroom Research*. Milton Keynes: Open University Press.

Meadows, S. (1996) *Parenting Behavior and Children's Cognitive Development*. Hove: Psychology Press.

Mitchell, D.E., Beach, S.A. and Baduruk, G. (1991) *Modelling the Relationship between Achievement and Class Size: A Re-analysis of the Tennessee Project STAR Data*. Riverside, CA: California Educational Research Co-operative.

Molnar, A., Smith, P., Zahorik, J., Palmer, A., Halbach, A. and Ehrle, K. (1999) Evaluating the SAGE program: a pilot program in targeted pupil–teacher reduction in Wisconsin, *Educational Evaluation and Policy Analysis*, 21(2): 165–77.

Moriarty, V., Edmonds, S., Blatchford, P. and Martin, C. (2001) Teaching young children: perceived satisfaction and stress, *Educational Research*, 43(1): 33–46.

Mortimore, P. and Blatchford, P. (1993) The issue of class size, in *National Commission on Education (1993) Briefings*. London: Heinemann.

Mortimore, P., Mortimore, J., Thomas, H., Cairns, R. and Taggart, B. (1992) *The Innovative Uses of Non-Teaching Staff in Primary Schools Project: Final Report*. London: Institute of Education/DfEE.

Mosteller, F. (1995) The Tennessee study of class size in the early grades, *The Future of Children – Critical Issues for Children and Youths*, 5(2): 113–27.

Moyles, J. with Suschitzky, W. (1997) *Jills of All Trades*. London: University of Leicester/Association of Teachers and Lecturers.

Muijs, D. and Reynolds, D. (2002) The effectiveness of the use of Learning Support Assistants in improving the mathematics achievement of low achieving pupils in primary school. Paper presented to International Congress for School Effectiveness and Improvement, Copenhagen.

Nye, B.A., Achilles, C.M., Zaharias, J.B, Fulton, B.D. and Wallenhorst, M.P. (1992) Small is far better. Paper presented to Mid-South Educational Research Association, Knoxville, TN.

Nye, B., Hedges, L.V. and Konstantopoulos, S. (2000) The effects of small classes on academic achievement: the results of the Tennessee class size experiment, *American Educational Research Journal*, 37(1): 123–51.

O'Donnell, A.M. and King, A. (eds) (1999) *Cognitive Perspectives on Peer Learning*. Mahwah, NJ: Erlbaum.

Ofsted (1995a). *Class Size and the Quality of Education*. London: HMSO.

Ofsted (1995b) *The Annual Report of Her Majesty's Chief Inspector of Schools, Standards and Quality in Education 1993/4*. London: HMSO.

Pan, H-L. and Yu, C. (1999) Educational reforms with their impacts on school effectiveness and school improvement in Taiwan, R.O.C. *School Effectiveness and School Improvement*, 10(1), 72–85.

Parker, J.G. and Asher, S.R. (1987) Peer relations and later personal adjustment: are low-accepted children at risk?, *Psychological Bulletin*, 102(3): 357–89.

Pate-Bain, H., Achilles, C.M., McKenna, B. and Zaharias, J. (1992) Class size makes a difference, *Phi Delta Kappa*, 74(3): 253–6.

Pellegrini, A. and Blatchford, P. (2000) *Children's Interactions at School: Peers and Teachers*. London: Edward Arnold.

Prais, S.J. (1996) Class size and learning: the Tennessee experiment – what follows?, *Oxford Review of Education*, 22: 399–414.

Rice, J.K. (1999) The impact of class size on instructional strategies and the use of time in High School mathematics and science courses, *Educational Evaluation and Policy Analysis*, 21(2): 215–29.

Rivkin, S.G., Hanushek, E.A. and Kain, J.F. (2000) Teachers, schools and achievement. Paper presented to Amherst College, University of Rochester, New York.

Rowe, K.J. (1995) Factors affecting students' progress in reading: key findings from a longitudinal study, *Literacy, Teaching and Learning*, 1(2): 57–110.

Rubin, K.H., Bukowski, W. and Parker, J. (1998) Peer interactions, relationships, and groups, in W. Damon (ed.) and N. Eisenberg (vol. ed.) *Handbook of Child Psychology: Volume 3: Social Emotional and Personality Development*. New York: John Wiley.

Shapson, S.M., Wright, E.N., Eason, G. and Fitzgerald, J. (1980) An experimental study of the effects of class size, *American Educational Research Journal*, 17: 144–52.

Shulman, L.S. (1986) Paradigms and research programs in the study of teaching, in M.C. Wittrock (ed.) *Handbook of Research on Teaching*, 3rd edn. New York: Macmillan.

Slavin, R.E. (1989) Class size and student achievement: small effects of small classes, *Educational Psychologist*, 24: 99–110.

Slavin, R.E. (1990) Class size and student achievement: is smaller better?, *Contemporary Education*, 62: 6–12.

Slavin, R.E., Harley, E.A. and Chamberlaine, A. (2000) *Co-operative Learning and Achievement: Research and Theory*. Baltimore, MD: Johns Hopkins University Press.

Smith, A.B., McMillan, B.W., Kennedy, S. and Ratcliffe, B. (1989) The effect of improving pre-school teacher/child ratios: an 'experiment in nature', *Early Child Development and Care*, 41: 123–38.

Smith, P.K. and Connolly, K. (1980) *The Ecology of Preschool Behaviour*. London: Cambridge University Press.

Swann, W., Hancock, R. and Marr, A. (2001) Variations in primary school classroom assistant employment. Paper presented to British Educational Research Association, Leeds, September.

Tharp, R. and Gallimore, R. (1991) A theory of teaching as assisted performance, in P. Light, S. Sheldon and M. Woodhead (eds) *Learning to Think*. London: Routledge.

Thompson, B. (1975) Adjustment to School Scale, *Educational Research*, 17(2): 128–36.

Tizard, B. and Hughes, M. (1984) *Young Children Learning.* London: Fontana.

Tizard, B., Blatchford, P. Burke, J., Farquhar, C. and Plewis, I. (1988) *Young Children at School in the Inner City.* Hove: Erlbaum.

Turner, C.M. (1990) Prime Time: a reflection, *Contemporary Education*, 62(1): 24–27.

Vincent, D., Crumpler, M. and de la Mare, M. (2000). *Reading Progress Test.* London: Hodder and Stoughton.

Wang, M.C. and Finn, J.D. (2000) (eds) *How Small Classes Help Teachers Do Their Best.* Philadelphia, PA: Temple University Center for Research in Human Development.

Webb, N.M. and Falivar, S. (1999) Developing group interaction in middle school mathematics in A.M. O'Donnell and A. King (eds) *Cognitive Perspectives on Peer Learning.* Mahwah, NJ: Erlbaum.

Webb, N.M., Baxter, G.P. and Thompson, L. (1997) Teachers' grouping in fifth grade science classrooms, *Elementary School Journal*, 98(2): 91–112.

Wells, G. (1986) *The Meaning Makers: Children Learning Language and Using Language to Learn.* Portsmouth, NH: Hodder and Stoughton.

Wood, D. (1998) *How Children Think and Learn*, 2nd edn. Oxford: Blackwell.

Wood, D. and Wood, H. (1996) Vygotsky, Tutoring and Learning, *Oxford Review of Education*, 22(1): 5–16.

Word, E.R., Johnston, J., Pate-Bain, H. and Fulton, B.D. (1990) *The State of Tennessee's Student/Teacher Achievement Ratio (STAR) Project: Technical Report 1985–90.* Nashville: Tennessee State University.

Index